Commercial and Industrial Internet of Things Applications with the Raspberry Pi

Prototyping IoT Solutions

Ioana Culic
Alexandru Radovici
Cristian Rusu

Apress®

Commercial and Industrial Internet of Things Applications with the Raspberry Pi: Prototyping IoT Solutions

Ioana Culic
Bucharest, Romania

Alexandru Radovici
Bucharest, Romania

Cristian Rusu
Bucharest, Romania

ISBN-13 (pbk): 978-1-4842-5295-6   ISBN-13 (electronic): 978-1-4842-5296-3
https://doi.org/10.1007/978-1-4842-5296-3

Managing Director, Apress Media LLC: Welmoed Spahr
Acquisitions Editor: Aaron Black
Development Editor: James Markham
Coordinating Editor: Jessica Vakili

Distributed to the book trade worldwide by Springer Science+Business Media New York, 233 Spring Street, 6th Floor, New York, NY 10013. Phone 1-800-SPRINGER, fax (201) 348-4505, e-mail orders-ny@springer-sbm.com, or visit www.springeronline.com. Apress Media, LLC is a California LLC and the sole member (owner) is Springer Science + Business Media Finance Inc (SSBM Finance Inc). SSBM Finance Inc is a **Delaware** corporation.

For information on translations, please e-mail rights@apress.com, or visit http://www.apress.com/rights-permissions.

Apress titles may be purchased in bulk for academic, corporate, or promotional use. eBook versions and licenses are also available for most titles. For more information, reference our Print and eBook Bulk Sales web page at http://www.apress.com/bulk-sales.

Any source code or other supplementary material referenced by the author in this book is available to readers on GitHub via the book's product page, located at www.apress.com/978-1-4842-5295-6. For more detailed information, please visit http://www.apress.com/source-code.

Printed on acid-free paper

Table of Contents

About the Authors..ix

About the Technical Reviewer xi

Introduction xiii

Chapter 1: Internet of Things Systems Overview 1

What Is the Industrial IoT? 1

    The IoT Characteristics 3

    The IoT Architecture 6

The IIoT Systems 8

    About SCADA 10

    From Prototyping to Industrial Systems 12

    Specific IIoT Characteristics 14

Edge Computing..16

    The Raspberry Pi As an Edge Device..17

    The Raspberry Pi in Industry 19

IoT Communication Protocols 22

    Low-Level Data Transmission Protocols...22

    Application-Level Protocols 26

Interfacing with the IoT System 28

    User Interface 28

    Physical Controls 30

    Platform Interface...30

Software for IoT Systems...32

    Software Characteristics 32

    Software Development 34

Summary...39

Further Reading 40

Chapter 2: Getting Started with the Raspberry Pi and Wyliodrin STUDIO 45

About the Raspberry Pi 47

About Wyliodrin STUDIO 50

Run Wyliodrin STUDIO 52

    Run Wyliodrin STUDIO Locally 52

    Run Wyliodrin STUDIO in the Browser 53

Connect the Raspberry Pi to Wyliodrin STUDIO....................................53

    Manual Setup 55

    Connect the Raspberry Pi to the Local Version of Wyliodrin STUDIO 56

    Connect the Raspberry Pi to Browser Version of Wyliodrin STUDIO 57

Overview of Wyliodrin STUDIO 60

Deploy Applications on the Raspberry Pi 62

Summary...67

Chapter 3: Smart Digital Signage System 69

Necessary Components 70

The Application Architecture 71

    Electron 72

The Application 73

    Source Code 73

    Installing the Necessary Libraries 79

    Run the Application 81

Connect to the Internet 83

Arrange the Interface 90

Summary 94

Chapter 4: Smart Soda Dispenser System 95

Necessary Components 96

Interactive Soda Dispenser 98

The main.js File 98

The User Interface 99

Install Required Modules 107

Building the Dispenser 109

The Schematic 109

The Application 111

Installing the Modules 113

Connecting the System to the Internet 113

Set Up Ubidots Account 114

Initialize Widget Values 115

Compute the Liquid Amount 117

Create the Dashboard 120

Summary 123

Chapter 5: Smart Advertising System 125

Necessary Components 127

Gathering Surrounding Information 128

Connect the Camera Module 129

Enable the Camera 130

The Code 131

Personalize the Content 137

    Set Up Microsoft Cognitive Services Account...137

    Process the Picture 140

    Personalize the Content...142

Remotely Update Source Pictures...145

    Create a Google Service Account 145

    Upload Files on Google Drive..148

    Integrate Google Drive API in the Application 150

Connect USB Camera..155

Monitor the Environment 156

Summary..161

Chapter 6: Smart Metering System Using an Industrial Server........163

Industrial Applications Architecture 164

Necessary Components 166

The Smart Power Plug Interface 167

    Set Up the HS110 Smart Power Plug Using the Kasa App...........................169

    Set Up the HS110 Smart Power Plug Using the Python SDK.......................169

Write the Power Plug Driver..176

The OPC UA Server...181

    OPC UA Variables..184

    The OPC UA Server 185

    OPC UA Commander..189

    ProSys OPC UA Client 191

The Smart Power Plug Driver..193

    Write the Energy Values...194

    Switch the Power Plug On and Off 201

Putting It All Together...205

Summary..207

Chapter 7: Data Storing and Processing..209

Necessary Components 210

Use MariaDB to Store Data 211

Install MariaDB 213

External Storage Setup.. 214

Set Up the Data Model.. 223

Upgrade to Use Multiple Smart Plugs 228

The OPC UA Data Model 229

The New Smart Plug Driver 234

Store the Information in the Database... 249

Summary... 264

Chapter 8: Data Plotting 265

Necessary Components 266

Getting Started.. 266

Install Docker 267

Install Grafana... 269

Add the MariaDB Data Source 274

The Dashboard 277

Summary... 285

Index...287

About the Authors

Ioana Culic is currently a PhD candidate in the field of Internet of Things and the cofounder of Wyliodrin, a company that offers educational and industrial IoT solutions. She is a Teaching Assistant at the Politehnica University of Bucharest, Romania, and has also been teaching IoT technologies to high school and university students at different events for the last 5 years. Despite the technical background, writing has always been Ioana's passion and she managed to mix the two. She has published several articles in magazines such as the *MagPi* and *Make:* and books on Internet of Things technologies.

Alexandru Radovici has a PhD in the field of mobile computing and works as an Assistant Professor at the Politehnica University of Bucharest, Romania, teaching subjects related to operating systems, compilers, and Internet of Things. Alexandru believes in the power of education and teaching is his passion, so 14 years ago he founded an NGO that focuses on organizing IT educational events. Alexandru is also the cofounder and CTO of Wyliodrin, being in touch with the latest IoT technologies.

Cristian Rusu received his MSc and PhD from the Politehnica University of Bucharest, Romania, in 2011 and 2012, respectively. He is currently a postdoctoral researcher with the Istituto Italiano di Tecnologia (IIT), Genoa, Italy, working on machine learning and big data, and their applications to real-world problems. His research interests include computer science and signal processing with applications to wireless communications, sparse representations, dictionary learning, machine learning, and numerical linear algebra. In the context of wireless communications, his interests focus on MIMO systems, mmWave, and UAV communication.

About the Technical Reviewer

Sai Yamanoor is an embedded systems engineer, working for an industrial gases company in Buffalo, New York. His interests, deeply rooted in DIY and open source hardware, include developing gadgets that aid behavior modification. He has published two books with his brother, and in his spare time he likes to contribute to build things that improve quality of life. You can find his project portfolio at `http://saiyamanoor.com`.

Introduction

During the last couple of years, the Internet of Things (IoT) has become a mature technology with applications both in the industrial and consumer markets. The IoT revolution promises to create ambient intelligence by connecting all the devices and objects around us and enabling them to adapt and behave following people's needs. A simple example would be a scenario in which the alarm clock is aware of the meeting you have at 9:00 AM and by taking into account the traffic conditions, it wakes you up at an appropriate hour, without you having to set it up the previous evening. Also, the coffee machine has already the coffee prepared for you, and other arrangements for the day are taken into consideration. While this scenario is still to be achieved, many technological advancements have been made in this direction. The result is a wide range of embedded hardware devices, various communication protocols with an accent on efficiency and security, and plenty of software platforms designed to manage all these resources.

One of the most popular hardware platforms for prototyping IoT applications is the Raspberry Pi. Hobbyists and students everywhere have been integrating it into IoT projects since 2012, when the first version was released. From controlling home lights to automatically feeding your pet, the Pi is present in many people's homes. However, few people think of it as something more than a prototyping or educational platform.

The purpose of this book is to give you a new perspective on how the Raspberry Pi can be used by integrating it into commercial or industrial applications that can be easily scaled and deployed as products.

Throughout the book, we will guide you through a series of practical examples that use the Raspberry Pi as the core around which fully developed products are built. We hope that after you follow all the examples, you will have a different view of how the Raspberry Pi or other similar devices can be used and have a complete perspective on how to move from prototyping a home device to building a fully scalable and marketable product.

Who This Book Is For

The book targets people passionate about building Internet of Things systems: from hobbyists to entrepreneurs, especially those who would like to start a business in this area. The notions presented are accessible to any person who has had some contact with the Raspberry Pi or some similar device and understands basic pin control operations. Some web development (HTTP and JavaScript/jQuery/Vue.js/Angular.js) experience is welcomed as this can help understand the presented concepts quicker. However, the projects are detailed step by step, so anybody with a basic understanding of programming can follow them. The final goal is to obtain several working IoT prototypes.

Technologies Used

All the chapters that describe applications are structured in a manner that outlines the necessary components of any successful IoT system: the hardware components, the software platform, and the connection to other devices and the Internet.

For the hardware aspect, besides the description of how to build and connect the components to the Raspberry Pi, we will also present the full connection schematic. Each chapter will also begin with a list of components necessary for building the project hardware.

On the software side, the applications that we build will consist of a user interface and application logic. The two are written using HTML and JavaScript technologies. For the User Interface (UI) control, we will integrate Vue.js as a framework built for easier and faster development of HTML-based user interfaces. To run the applications on the Raspberry Pi, we will integrate them with the Electron framework.

The Internet connection component will be addressed by incorporating a web API into the applications. In each chapter, we will present a different web service (e.g., social network interaction, weather information, or image processing) that is a vital component of the overall system and which delivers the specific IoT flavor to the application.

Necessary Hardware

This book aims to present the essential IoT technologies in a very practical manner. As a result, each chapter guides the reader through building a prototype of an IoT application, requiring specific hardware components to be connected to the Raspberry Pi.

To help you prepare implement the applications presented throughout the book, we created a list with the necessary hardware:

- Raspberry Pi

- HDMI display

- Touchscreen display

- 3KY-019 relays or similar

- Three water pumps

- 5V power source

- Raspberry Pi camera module or USB camera

- PIR motion sensor

- Breadboard

- Jumper wires

- TP-Link HS110 Smart Power Plug (preferably two)

- Raspberry Pi PoE HAT (optional)

- A PoE (802.3af) capable network switch or PoE injector (optional)

- External hard drive or SSD drive (optional, a USB 3.0 device is recommended)

To successfully implement the applications, you do not need to acquire the same hardware components. Many of them can be replaced with other similar hardware. This is why we recommend you do a short analysis of the required equipment and other available options before you get started.

Topics Covered

Chapter 1 introduces the Internet of Things field and the basic architecture of IoT applications. We present the main characteristics of commercial and industrial IoT systems by emphasizing the transition from prototyping to building production applications.

Chapter 2 gives an overview of existing development environments for building IoT systems and guides the reader through the setup process required to connect the Raspberry Pi to Wyliodrin STUDIO.

Chapter 3 introduces basic concepts such as creating a user interface-based IoT system and how to include the "Internet" component into your applications. The final result is a web-based IoT platform that displays the current weather conditions.

Chapter 4 guides the reader through building a smart soda dispenser using HTML and Vue.js. We also emphasize the importance of remotely monitoring the deployed systems and how we can achieve this.

Chapter 5 focuses on integrating picture and video capabilities into IoT solutions. We present the Pi Camera module and how to control it so we can build a smart advertising system that adapts the commercials to the current audience.

Chapter 6 introduces industrial technologies, focusing on how to use the OPC UA protocol to control smart home systems, in our case, a power plug.

Chapter 7 focuses on the implementation of the OPC UA industrial communications protocol. In this case, we expand the project implemented in Chapter 6, so data from multiple power plugs is systematically gathered using this protocol.

Chapter 8, the final chapter, introduces open source technologies for data plotting and visualization, by enhancing the project developed in Chapter 7.

CHAPTER 1

Internet of Things Systems Overview

In this chapter, we provide a general outline of the Internet of Things (IoT) with a particular focus on the commercial and industrial aspects. We cover the basic terminology and technologies surrounding the IoT, its history, and current state of the art, including all its main components: hardware devices, software development, and communication protocols.

What Is the Industrial IoT?

The main idea behind the Internet of Things is to interconnect electronic systems that can sense or interact with the environment and communicate among themselves. While the typical examples of IoT include everyday objects and applications, the principles of the IoT can also be applied to commercial and industrial systems leading to better results and improved efficiency. Therefore, as part of the IoT, we encounter the specific notion of the Industrial Internet of Things (IIoT) referring to commercial and industrial products.

While the industrial and consumer markets address different needs and propose different solutions and products, when it comes to building an IoT system, the fundamental characteristics and architectures are based on a set of common principles. These are the principles we explore in this chapter.

© Ioana Culic; Alexandru Radovici; Cristian Rusu 2020
I. Culic et al., *Commercial and Industrial Internet of Things Applications with the Raspberry Pi*,
https://doi.org/10.1007/978-1-4842-5296-3_1

First, let us introduce some basic definitions for the IoT and IIoT.

While there is no unique definition for the IoT (see, e.g., the IEEE "the ever-changing definition of the IoT"[1]), we choose to present the following description provided by the Internet Engineering Task Force (IETF) in 2010.

> *The basic idea is that IoT will connect objects around us (electronic, electrical, non-electrical) to provide seamless communication and contextual services provided by them. Development of RFID tags, sensors, actuators, mobile phones makes it possible to materialize IoT which interact and co-operate each other to make the service better and accessible anytime, from anywhere.*
>
> —Internet Engineering Task Force

We also give a description of the *thing* in the Internet of Things.

> *In the vision of IoT, "things" are very various such as computers, sensors, people, actuators, refrigerators, TVs, vehicles, mobile phones, clothes, food, medicines, books, etc. These things are classified as three scopes: people, machine (for example, sensor, actuator, etc.) and information (for example, clothes, food, medicine, books, etc.). These "things" should be identified at least by one unique way of identification for the capability of addressing and communicating with each other and verifying their identities. In here, if the "thing" is identified, we call it the "object."*
>
> —Internet Engineering Task Force

---

[1]https://iot.ieee.org/definition.html

When it comes to the IIoT, we choose the description by HP.[2]

The IIoT consists of internet-connected machinery and the advanced analytics platforms that process the data they produce. IIoT devices range from tiny environmental sensors to complex industrial robots. While the word "industrial" may call to mind warehouses, shipyards and factory floors, IIoT technologies hold a lot of promise for a diverse range of industries, including agriculture, healthcare, financial services, retail, and advertising.

The Industrial Internet of Things is a subcategory of the Internet of Things, which also includes consumer-facing applications such as wearable devices, smart home technology, and self-driving cars. Sensor-embedded devices, machines, and infrastructure that transmit data via the Internet and are managed by software are the hallmark of both concepts.

—HP

The IoT Characteristics

Given these basic definitions, let us now discuss some essential characteristics of the IoT. The focus of an IoT system falls on the *things* on top of which it is built. Any IoT solution aims to bring intelligence to already existing objects/devices and enable them to behave autonomously. The *intelligence* of such a solution is based on sensing and action, connectivity, collection of large amounts of data, and processing and storage capabilities, resulting in the following essential characteristics of an IoT system:

- Connectivity – This is the basis of any IoT solution; sensors are connected between them selves and to devices; devices are connected to each other and to the Internet; be it at a local or a global level, the capacity to exchange data is the driving force behind the IoT.

---

[2]www.hpe.com/emea_europe/en/what-is/industrial-iot.html

- Management of the things – The purpose of any IoT device is to sense and interact with the environment, and this can be done only through physical objects, which we generically call things.

- Heterogeneity –The IoT ecosystem is built on top of various hardware devices, network infrastructures, and processing platforms that need to exchange information and act toward a common goal.

- Data collection – The intelligence of the IoT systems is based on the data that sensors gather; this data is processed, and then the data is converted to actionable information.

- Dynamism – The IoT infrastructures are changing continuously, networks adjust parameters dynamically, sensors can connect and disconnect, devices can enter idle, awake, or sleep modes, and the systems need to maintain their correct behavior, independent of the occurring changes in the environment.

- Large-scale – As of 2020, the number of devices connected to the Internet is approximated to reach 20 billion,[3] and it increases at an exponential rate; this requires infrastructure and platforms capable of managing such a high number of connections.

---

[3]www.gartner.com/en/newsroom/press-releases/2017-02-07-gartner-says-8-billion-connected-things-will-be-in-use-in-2017-up-31-percent-from-2016

- Autonomy – Many of the intelligent devices designed are meant to be deployed in remote places; in this case, the devices have to make decisions without human intervention while they might not have access to a continuous power source, depending on batteries or alternative sources of energy. Simultaneously these devices need to be remotely monitored, controlled and even updated or repaired.

- Privacy and security – These are one of the biggest concerns regarding the IoT. Connecting heating systems or health devices to the Internet exposes them to significant risks; gaining compromising or malicious control over such a system can have disastrous consequences. Equally important, the IoT users need to understand (and agree) what data is collected at all times.

Consider an IoT smart building system that monitors the temperature inside the building and has access to the inhabitants' calendars. Based on this data, it can ensure that when people arrive or are already at home their preferred environment temperature is set, while when they are away, it can optimize the heating and cooling systems to reduce energy consumption and costs. Such a system needs to interconnect temperature sensors to Heating, Ventilation, and Air Conditioning (HVAC) systems and also retrieve data about the inhabitants' location. Also, for the system to be effective, it needs to behave autonomously and uninterrupted and ensure that data concerning the users' behavior is securely stored and manipulated. Since information about the location of the inhabitants has to be available to the system, privacy and security concerns take center stage. For example, unauthorized access to this information might tell burglars exactly when the home is empty. We can quickly identify many of the previously mentioned characteristics in this simple example.

An essential requirement for the success of the IoT is that people need to be comfortable and secure when using new technologies. Unfortunately, IoT technologies have also introduced new specific security concerns and risks. If all the devices that surround us are connected to the Internet, then a security breach might result in real-world damage to both property and humans. One of the worst modern IoT security concerns is the use of *botnets*. A botnet is a collection of devices whose security has been compromised and is used by a third party that controls it to perform cyberattacks against a particular target. Usually, the attacks take the form of Distributed Denial-of-Service (DDoS). The IoT is particularly susceptible to such an attack because of the large number of devices connected to the IoT networks. Two recent prominent attacks were the 2016 Mirai[4] and Remaiten[5] botnets.

The IoT Architecture

Generally, an IoT solution has the following behavior: it senses the environment, analyzes the gathered data, and reacts based on the conclusions. To better illustrate the components of a generic IoT system and the way they interact with each other, specialists have introduced the IoT stack. Since the IoT is still profoundly lacking standardization, there are various versions of the stack, more or less detailed, with a focus on different aspects. Nonetheless, from a broad perspective, most of them consist of the following components:

- Sensors and actuators

- Local processing and storage

- Network and Internet connection

- Cloud processing

---

[4]https://securityintelligence.com/news/leaked-mirai-malware-boosts-iot-insecurity-threat-level/

[5]www.securityweek.com/new-remaiten-malware-builds-botnet-linux-based-routers

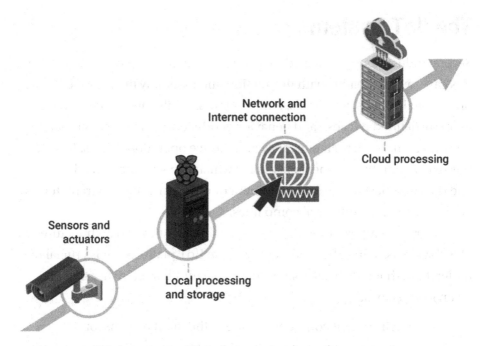

Figure 1-1. *The Internet of Things stack*

Based on Figure 1-1, we notice that the *sensors and actuators* are placed at the bottom of the stack, as they are the ones communicating directly with the environment. Up the stack, we place the local processing and storage devices, also called *edge devices*. These are computers such as a Raspberry Pi, which are capable of exchanging information with the peripherals and have minimal computing capabilities so they can preprocess the data received from the sensors. On the upper level, edge devices can be connected to network devices such as routers and have access to the *Internet*. Finally, at the top of the stack, there is the *cloud*, where large amounts of data coming from a multitude of edge devices are stored and, with the help of machine learning and artificial intelligence (AI), can be leveraged to reach important decisions and perform complex analyses or predictions of future systems and human behaviors.

The IIoT Systems

Several industries are expected to be the biggest beneficiaries of the IoT. In this case, we are dealing with production and assembly lines, oil wells, photovoltaic plants, windmills, among others. While these systems have a clearly defined purpose and behavior, producers are in constant search for ways to increase their efficiency and reduce operational costs. It is for this reason that the prospect of systems which can self-analyze, adapt, and optimize based on the environment or other third-party parameters is appealing to most industrial companies.

So far, we have explored the generic characteristics and architectures of IoT systems. While these also apply to the IIoT platforms, it is crucial to understand that industrial systems have specific characteristics that are taken into account:

- Environment conditions – One of the main reasons for building autonomous industrial machines is because in many cases the working conditions in factories are not favorable to humans as they can be exposed to chemical substances, high temperatures, or extreme humidity leading to long-term health problems.

- Costs – All companies have the goal to be as economically efficient as possible, and therefore the operational costs are an important decision factor when introducing new systems or devices in production or assembly lines.

- Downtime – The activities carried out in plants are usually uninterrupted, apart from specific, limited amounts of time when maintenance is done. Of course, there are exceptions as systems might break down, but in this case, any downtime may be translated into critical financial losses.

Based on these characteristics, any IoT solution implemented in the industry has to meet the following requirements:

- Robustness – Any industrial product has to be adapted to the environment where it will be deployed. It needs to withstand harsh working conditions, and this is why most of the devices designed for industrial use are *ruggedized*.

- Stability – Having a device that behaves unusually or breaks unexpectedly results in downtime; many industrial devices are required to work continuously (sometimes close to their technical limits) for potentially long periods.

- Real-time – Some of the machines deployed in factories need to respond very quickly to triggers or events in the environment. Response times are essential to ensure accurate readings and results and the overall synchronization of the system resources.

A survey carried out in 2015 by Morgan Stanley and *Automation World* magazine has outlined that the main incentive for the adoption of the Industrial Internet of Things (IIoT) is the desire to improve operational efficiency, followed by the desire to improve productivity.[6]

One of the first steps toward making a process more efficient and productive is to analyze its current status and find ways to improve. This need explains the broad adoption of IoT technologies in the industrial market. The main characteristic of the IoT systems is that they use sensors to gather information about the environment, making them suitable for helping increase productivity and reduce costs. Besides the big data and analytics aspect of the IoT, regularly monitoring industrial equipment

---

[6]www.i-scoop.eu/internet-of-things-guide/industrial-internet-things-iiot-saving-costs-innovation/

using sensors can provide more accurate data compared to the measures carried out by humans. The goal is to enable early detection of machine deterioration and help prevent unexpected failures, reducing costs related to maintenance and downtime.

The historical need to increase the operational efficiency of industrial processes has led to several monitoring and control solutions being developed, the predecessors to the current IIoT platforms.

About SCADA

Historically, the IIoT is not the first attempt to improve and modernize the industrial infrastructure.

Supervisory Control and Data Acquisition (SCADA) is an industrial control system developed in the 1950s. The system is designed to be integrated into factories' infrastructures and enables the monitoring and control of the industrial operations. SCADA has been used extensively in industries such as energy, manufacturing, oil and gas, transportation, waste management, food, and many others. Today, SCADA systems are still in widespread use to manage traffic flow and regulate traffic lights. Over time, SCADA systems have been continuously improved across four technological generations: the initial monolith structure, the distributed and networked phases, and finally their evolution to modern IIoT systems.[7]

SCADA systems use sensors that retrieve data such as temperature, humidity, or vibration about the industrial machines and display it in a user interface with the help of graphs and other visual elements. On the other side, the system is also connected to valves, motors, pumps, and other control mechanisms that can be managed from the same user interface without the need for direct human intervention on the industrial machine. Also, factory employees can design routines, so a system responds automatically to changes in the environment. For instance, we can

---

[7]www.engineersgarage.com/articles/scada-systems

program a machine to shut down if some system parameters (e.g., temperature) reaches a certain level deemed critical.

SCADA can also be deployed across large interconnected industrial systems, leading us to the question of *how is SCADA different from modern Industrial IoT solutions?*

While SCADA brings centralized monitoring and control over the industrial platforms, it lacks the intelligence specific to IoT systems; more precisely, it lacks the cloud component of the IoT stack. This, in turn, limits the system to take simple, local decisions. Even worse, historically, these decisions were made often by human operators introducing the possibility of errors. It is for this reason that many producers of industrial IoT platforms decide to extend the SCADA infrastructure and bring machine learning and AI capabilities and remove human operators from the loop.

As two of the significant incidents of the twentieth century, Three Mile Island and Chernobyl disasters also involved human operator errors, the hope is that AI capabilities will be able to eliminate or at least drastically reduce the future risks of such destructive events.

Also, one of the most significant disadvantages of SCADA is security, or more precisely the lack of it. Since it was designed when platforms were not connected to any external system, security breaches were unlikely to happen. Today, SCADA relies on the mechanism of security through obscurity (design and implementation secrecy), which the latest discovered vulnerabilities such as Spectre and Meltdown prove to be inefficient. A now-infamous security breach example is the 2010 attack called Stuxnet on Iranian industrial facilities when attackers were able to log into the SCADA database and steals design and control files.[8] A more recent and less spectacular but equally important example is the hacking of traffic systems in large cities.[9]

---

[8]http://archive.is/20120525053210/http://www.computerworld.com/s/article/print/9185419/Siemens_Stuxnet_worm_hit_industrial_systems?tax onomyName=Network+Security&taxonomyId=142

[9]https://resources.infosecinstitute.com/hacking-traffic-light-systems

From Prototyping to Industrial Systems

The first step when building an IoT product is to prototype it, and here we can take advantage of how popular the IoT is among the engineering, maker, and hobbyist communities. There are plenty of IoT books, magazines, and events dedicated to the do-it-yourself (DIY) community, and a simple online search leads to thousands of tutorials on how to build your connected lighting system or how to make your vacuum cleaner smart. However, once the proof of concept is up and running, there are a few additional aspects to be taken into account until the device can actually be sold and even deployed in an industrial environment:

- Stability – It is important to ensure that the system works without any unexpected interruptions, and if an error occurs, the device should be able to recover without external intervention. Although for a prototype, you can afford to have some errors or crashes during the testing phase, when it comes to commercial and industrial devices, having a product that stops running can cost your client a lot and can cost you a client. Before releasing it into mass production, it is vital to thoroughly test the device and consider all the possible use cases.

- Certifications – For a product to be sold on the market, it has to have precise specifications and pass quality verifications, a process called *certification*. After the device passes the quality tests, it is certified to be used in a specific region. This is because different countries have different requirements (e.g., the Federal Communications Commission FCC in the United States, the European Economic Area CE marking, etc.). Therefore, after you build the prototype, you need to ensure that it does not consume too much energy, performs accurate readings with specified uncertainty, does not interfere with other (especially wireless) devices also in the environment, does not emit chemical substances in the environment, and has no risk of exploding or harming humans.

- Support and warranty – Although you already tested the device and the risk of it crashing is minimal, it still exists. For this reason, you need to search for ways in which you can offer support for the system you deployed. This is not necessarily easy as you need to search for ways to remotely diagnose the product and, if possible, remotely repair it. This is necessary because shipping the device back in service has high costs, and if the device is a smart fridge, it may be impossible to ask the customer to ship it back, so you will have to send a technician if there is no way to fix the product remotely.

- Updates – Once the solution reaches the customer, you need to provide software updates for new features and security requirements. It would help if you assured your clients that the product they bought would function appropriately for a certain amount of time, and this also implies that it is not exposed to new security breaches. It is crucial to have the means to push the updates remotely and ensure that there are no failures and no risks of *bricking* the device.

- Endurance – When it comes to industrial devices, you need to ensure they can withstand harsh working conditions for an extended amount of time. This implies that the components you use have to be more resistant and finally have the whole device ruggedized, so it is not directly exposed to the environment.

- Safety and Security – These are some of the most
  important aspects of any IoT system. Both commercial
  and industrial IoT platforms collect and manipulate
  sensitive data and control delicate peripherals. In this
  context, there are multiple aspects where a security
  breach can expose users to great perils. Also, when
  talking about industrial devices, the costs and the
  risks are even higher (e.g., an assembly line that
  stops working for 5 minutes can generate millions
  of dollars in losses, secret industrial data might be
  stolen). Therefore, before deploying an IoT system
  into production, it is very important to keep in
  mind all components and how each of them can be
  viciously manipulated. While a perfectly safe system is
  impossible to design, it is crucial to implement multiple
  and various security mechanisms that make it very
  difficult for a malicious person to take control over it.

Specific IIoT Characteristics

While the IIoT is an extension of the IoT, and therefore it borrows most
of its fundamental concepts from the IoT, there are several technologies
uniquely developed in the commercial and industrial environments:

- Digital twins[10] are digital replicas of physical systems. The
  purpose of these twins is to simulate, optimize, and test in
  real-time the physical systems. A prominent example is
  the use of digital twins in the context of smart buildings.[11]

---

[10]A. El Saddik. *Digital Twins: The convergence of multimedia technologies.* IEEE
MultiMedia, 25(2): 87–92, 2018

[11]www.ibm.com/blogs/internet-of-things/creating-buildings-digital-twin/

- Radio-frequency identification (RFID)[12] uses electromagnetic fields to automatically identify and track electronic tags attached to physical objects or implanted in animals (livestock and pets). The RFID tags make it possible to identify and monitor the things of the IoT network efficiently.

- Edge intelligence[13] refers to the ability of a system to collect, process data from sensors, and make decisions in the environment locally, without sending the data to the cloud. The point of this technology is to increase the efficiency of the system by reducing latency, costs, and security risks just by avoiding unnecessary communications to the cloud.

- Smart (or predictive) maintenance[14] refers to technologies that allow for the monitoring of in-service equipment with the purpose of estimating when maintenance should be performed. The goal of this technology is to increase productivity (also boosting "just-in-time manufacturing") and reduce costs associated with equipment downtime.

---

[12]www.atlasrfidstore.com/rfid-beginners-guide/

[13]www.hpe.com/emea_europe/en/what-is/intelligent-edge.html

[14]R. Keith Mobley. *An Introduction to Predictive Maintenance*. Butterworth-Heinemann, 2002

- Electronic Logging Device (ELD or E-Log)[15] is an electronic hardware device that is attached to another machine in order to log its activities. The classic example is the logging device attached to motor vehicles in order to record driving hours. More broadly, digital logging devices are able to provide real-time monitoring and diagnosis information about any system.

Edge Computing

Edge computing is a paradigm of the IoT in which primary data processing and decisions are made at the second level of the IoT stack. While this does not wholly exclude the cloud component from an IoT solution, the edge computing model aims to leverage the processing and storage capabilities of devices such as the Raspberry Pi (or other edge devices) and offload the cloud from ineffective operations.

Most of the IoT solutions that were developed at the onset of the IoT revolution used to rely exclusively on cloud processing and storage capabilities. The general functioning principle would involve data to be gathered from the sensors, sent to the cloud, which would generate all decisions and send back the necessary actions to the actuators. In this context, the cloud was overwhelmed by a large amount of redundant data and processing. Security and privacy concerns have also been raised due to external data exposure.

The solution proposed by the edge computing principle is to do basic data processing on the devices that gather the readings from the sensors and even take local decisions based on the information they retrieve. In this case, the edge devices would filter the readings and send to the cloud only the relevant values. Furthermore, the cloud would be used only for processing that requires powerful computational resources such as machine learning and AI.

---

[15]www.eldfacts.com/eld-facts/

To better understand the advantages of edge computing, let us take the example of a wind turbine control solution. The system can measure wind speed and change the turbine's pace accordingly. Without edge computing, this solution would measure the wind speed every second and send the (mostly identical) readings to the cloud, resulting in large amounts of redundant data to be transmitted and stored. Next, when the readings would change, the cloud would send the commands to adapt the turbine rotation speed. In the edge computing paradigm, the readings are stored on the edge device, and only variations are sent to the cloud, significantly reducing the amount of transmitted data. Also, the edge device has the processing capability to take basic decisions and command the wind turbine to change its pace. On the other side, the cloud can be used to gather the relevant data from a multitude of turbines in different places, and by using advanced algorithms, it can predict natural phenomena such as storms or even tornados and optimize the long-term functioning of the turbine.

In the current context of having sensors and connected devices increasing at an exponential pace resulting in vast amounts of data and much processing, edge computing is gaining more and more popularity, and the majority of new IoT platforms rely on this model.

The Raspberry Pi As an Edge Device

As of 2020, the Raspberry Pi is the most used edge device for building IoT solutions among the DIY and maker communities. The affordable price and accessibility made it extremely popular. The computing and storage capabilities of the Raspberry Pi enables people to use it as an edge device within the IoT projects they are building.

For the hobbyist, the Raspberry Pi comes in two main flavors: the full model and the Raspberry Pi zero model. While the complete model has all the basic features of a modern computer (Wi-Fi, BLE, Ethernet port, HDMI port, USB port, stereo output jack port, etc.), the Raspberry Pi zero family was designed as a smaller, cheaper alternative having fewer connectors and fewer features. Also, both Raspberry Pi models can be directly connected to sensors and actuators through pins. The devices can support the basic GPIO, SPI, I2C, serial connections, and other more complex types.

Besides the devices we mentioned, the Raspberry Pi Foundation also released a compute module, built for industrial use. The Raspberry Pi Compute Module family consists of devices having the same core (processor, memory, etc.) as the previous, but with a different form factor. The core modules have reduced dimensions and are designed to be integrated into custom systems. Therefore, they support more GPIO and other interfaces that are intended to be connected to external modules.

Figure 1-2 depicts a Raspberry Pi Compute Module 3+. The device has the following main specifications:

- Broadcom, Cortex-A53 64-bit SoC processor, running at 1.2GHz.

- 1GB LPDDR2 SDRAM memory.

- Depending on the model it can have 8GB/16GB/32GB of eMMC flash memory.

- Board dimensions: 67.6 × 31.1 × 3.7 mm.

Figure 1-2. *The Raspberry Pi Compute Module 3+[16]*

---

[16]www.raspberrypi.org/products/compute-module-3/

Given its characteristics and the variety of projects and products built on top of it, it would be an understatement to refer to the Raspberry Pi only as a prototyping device. The Raspberry Pi is widely integrated into commercial and industrial machines. However, as the device still lacks some characteristics that are very important for the industrial system, it requires external hardware and software to make it suitable for industrial environments.

The Raspberry Pi in Industry

A fundamental characteristic of any industrial system is the need to respond in real time to specific triggers. This means that the machine has a well-defined maximum amount of time during which it needs to react to an environment parameter change or event. As a result, a real-time system has strict constraints related to the timing at which instructions are executed. If you think of an assembly line, each robot needs to be perfectly synchronized with its peers and carry out its actions in a determined amount of time. Similarly, the reaction time of the system has to be below some prescribed value (usually expressed in milliseconds) in order to be useful. To achieve these requirements, real-time systems usually run only one piece of software to ensure certainty regarding when each line of code gets to be executed.

As already mentioned, industrial devices need to be robust and to work uninterrupted for long periods of time (years) in harsh conditions (strong vibrations, high temperatures, humidity, and high levels of harmful chemical substances). If, or when, they fail, IoT devices need to be able to reset and recover automatically or, as in the case of catastrophic failures, send diagnosis information to the main systems. This is why most of the industrial systems are built around PLCs.

Programmable logic controllers (PLC) are ruggedized industrial computers designed to be integrated into systems such as manufacturing or assembly lines, robot devices, etc. They are computers specialized in controlling specific industrial processes. The processing unit is usually a microcontroller that runs its firmware, which is capable of real-time operations. Also, the device exposes robust connectors, resistant to tampering and short-circuits. PLCs are usually built as modular cases that can be easily integrated into the existing infrastructure and present a simple control and monitor interface, generally consisting of a display, status LEDs, switches, and buttons. Figure 1-3 depicts an example of a PLC device.

Today, PLCs which are compatible with the Raspberry exist, enabling the integration of the Raspberry Pi into industrial products. This way, companies willing to build systems that have a Raspberry Pi as a core component do not need to spend resources on building their custom hardware or ruggedizing the hardware device.

These devices come in robust casings that completely enclose the Raspberry Pi. They connect to the device's pins and expose industrial-grade connectors and peripherals, for example, LEDs or switches.

Another aspect that does not make the Raspberry Pi suitable for direct use inside industrial machines is the power supply. The Raspberry Pi needs to be connected to 5V DC, while the industrial systems usually work with higher voltages. This is why the hardware expansions also expose power sockets supporting voltages up to 30–40V DC as the Raspberry Pi receives current from the expansion.

Figure 1-3. *The APB Programmable Logic Controller*[17]

Examples of devices that are industrial expansions for the original Raspberry Pi are the Monarco Hat,[18] the Iono Pi,[19] the Revolution Pi,[20] or the UniPi.[21]

---

[17]www.circuitspecialists.com/apb-12mrdl.html

[18]www.monarco.io

[19]www.sferalabs.cc/iono-pi

[20]https://revolution.kunbus.com

[21]https://www.unipi.technology

IoT Communication Protocols

An electronic device that works in isolation collecting data and acting upon the environment is not considered a modern IoT device. The ability to communicate with other IoT devices and the cloud is essential to creating the type of interconnected world promised by the IoT.

In the context of heterogeneous devices having to interact with each other, the IoT relies on protocols that enable peripherals and devices to communicate. This is why a strong emphasis is placed on how data is transmitted between the components of an IoT system.

Next, we explore some of the most popular communications protocols currently used in IoT systems.

Low-Level Data Transmission Protocols

Be it *intra-board* (peripherals-to-device) or *inter-board* (device-to-device) communication, IoT systems require reliable and efficient ways of data transmission. One of the first aspects of data exchange between devices is the transmission medium, where we have two options: wired or wireless connections.

The main advantage of wired connections is that data transmission is done fast, reliably, and securely. On the other hand, if the system covers a large area to be monitored, wires have to stretch for long distances, making them prone to damage and failure. This is where wireless solutions might become necessary.

Many modern IoT devices are capable of wireless communications. Unfortunately, the transmission is not as fast and reliable as the wired lines. On the other hand, wireless solutions are useful for systems covering a large area: smart building solutions, in agriculture where crops and farms need to be monitored, or remote oil and gas extraction plants.

Some of the most popular intra-board wired protocols for commercial devices are:

- Universal Asynchronous Receiver/Transmitter
  (UART) – This protocol enables two devices to
  communicate using two lines for data transfer: transmit
  (TX) and receive (RX). Each device sends its streams of
  data on one line and reads incoming bits on the other
  line. Data is sent in packets delimited by start and end
  bits. There is no synchronization mechanism between
  the two devices. When one device detects the start
  sequence, it begins reading the data up until it detects
  the end sequence.

- Inter-Integrated Circuit (I^2C or I2C) – This transmission
  mechanism also uses two lines of communication: SDA
  (serial data) and SCL (serial clock). The SDA line is for
  the actual data transmission, while the other is only
  for the clock signal. The protocol has a bus topology
  and uses the master-slave architecture where only the
  master devices can initiate communication with the
  slaves. When connecting sensors to the Raspberry Pi,
  the device acts as the master, and the peripherals are
  the slaves. Also, unlike the UART, this protocol supports
  multiple masters connected to multiple slaves. When
  the master initiates data transmission, it also specifies
  the slave that it wants to communicate with. This
  information is sent to all peripherals so that only
  addressed slaves can prepare to send and receive data.

- Serial Peripheral Interface (SPI) – This transmission
  mechanism uses at least three lines of communication:
  Master Output/Slave Input (MOSI), Master Input/Slave
  Output (MISO), Clock (SCLK). It has a bus topology
  and also uses the master–slave architecture, allowing
  for multiple slaves connected to only one master.

In this case, SPI uses one extra line for each slave, the Slave Select/Chip Select (SS/CS). When the master wants to communicate with one of the slaves, this receives a LOW signal on the SS/CS line and becomes active. All the other slaves receive HIGH on the SS/CS line and become inactive (the behavior will be as if they were not connected to the communication lines). The actual data is transmitted on two lines. One line is for data sent by the master, while another line is for data sent from the slaves. The SCLK line is used for synchronization, and the SS lines that connect to only one slave enable the master to initiate the communication with a specific slave. The main advantage of SPI is that data is sent continuously, not in packets, and supports higher transmission rates. Also, the slave and master can simultaneously send data.

In industrial systems, communication is usually done via Ethernet connections, making the architecture scalable and modular. For the industry, the protocols designed on top of Ethernet, need to ensure reliability and fast transmission rates. Two of the most used industrial inter-board protocols are:

- Ethernet/IP – It is currently one of the most used industrial communication protocols. Depending on the purpose of communication, data can be transmitted either by UDP (real-time critical data coming from sensors or controlling actuators, where some data losses are acceptable) or by TCP (application parameters or other non-real-time information, where some data losses are unacceptable). Communication can be done through various mechanisms such as pooling, triggers, or direct unicast or multicast connections.

- Profinet – Profinet is an industrial protocol which aims to enable fast communication between industrial peripherals and control systems. It is built using an advanced synchronization mechanism that makes it efficient and allows real-time data transmission. Data packets are assigned priorities allocation of different bandwidth sizes.

As we previously mentioned, some IoT systems are easier to implement using wireless sensors. Therefore, a wide variety of wireless protocols, specially designed for edge devices have been developed. These protocols are built to ensure reliable and fast data transmission, using limited resources. Some of the wireless protocols used for commercial and industrial IoT systems are:

- Bluetooth Low Energy (BLE) – BLE is a protocol that uses radio frequencies for data transmission. It was first developed for smartphones, but due to its characteristics, it is currently supported by various sensors and integrated into edge devices. Despite its name, BLE is different from classical Bluetooth. BLE is designed to use low energy levels. As a result, the protocol supports small packets of data being transmitted at specific time intervals. Also, the information sent over BLE cannot cover large distances. All these characteristics are in contrast to Bluetooth, which does not balance energy consumption.

- LoRa – It is a protocol designed to be used for long-range communication. LoRa specifications state that data can be transmitted on distances of around 10km. In addition, LoRa is designed to consume very little energy, allowing battery-powered devices to run for years without the need to change the battery. Due to these characteristics, LoRa is heavily implemented into agricultural solutions that need to cover large areas.

- Zigbee – Zigbee is designed to be used for data transmission over small distances with very low energy consumption. With a transmission rate of around 250kb/s, the protocol is not tailored for systems requiring fast communication between devices. Zigbee was built especially for home automation systems, where the area to be covered is limited, and the communication speed is not crucial.

Application-Level Protocols

All the previously described protocols handle how information is transferred between devices and focus on ensuring data integrity and transport efficiency. The transfer specifications are implemented by the hardware devices used for the transmission. Most of the software logic is performed either in the lower-level libraries for microcontrollers or the operating system for higher-level systems.

As lower-level protocols make sure data is transmitted from one device to another, applications running on those devices must make sense of the data they are sending or receiving. As several applications need to exchange data, application-level protocols have also been defined. Consider them just a set of standards and rules that applications enforce to understand the data they exchange. These protocols are based on and run on top of the lower-level communication protocols previously described.

At the application level, we can choose from several protocols designed to support fast and efficient communication, usually based on small-sized data packets (as sensor readings are usually short).

The protocols most used for inter-device communication for nonindustrial pieces of equipment are

- MQ Telemetry Transport (MQTT) – MQTT is a lightweight protocol implemented over TCP/IP based on the publish–subscribe paradigm. The publisher broadcasts messages based on different topics, and subscribers receive all messages related to the topic they subscribed to. It was designed to enable communication between constrained devices over limited bandwidth networks. MQTT packets are reduced in size: maximum message payload is 256MB. MQTT ensures three different levels of QoS for data transmission. While level 1 works on the *fire and forget* principle, levels 2 and 3 ensure that each packet reaches its destination.

- Constraint Application Protocol (CoAP) – CoAP is a protocol designed for devices with limited capabilities and unreliable, constrained networks as well. CoAP is built in a similar way to HTTP, making use of the same request methods: GET, POST, PUT, etc. On the other hand, the CoAP packets are much smaller as the header format is different from HTTP.

For industrial machines, the most common communication is done using the following technologies:

- Modbus – It is an application-level protocol and can be implemented on top of several transport layers such as serial, Ethernet, or Wi-Fi. It was developed in 1979 and is currently one of the most used communication technologies. Due to its versatility, it is now one of the most implemented communication protocols in the industry and is used for both device-to-device and peripherals-to-device communications. Modbus is based on the client-server paradigm. While over serial connections, one specific device is assigned the master role, over Ethernet any device can initiate the communication. There are several versions of the Modbus protocol, each with different packet formats.

- OPC Unified Architecture (OPC-UA) – It is built on top of the TCP/IP stack and is based on a service-oriented architecture. In this case, the device implementing the OPC-UA protocol exposes functions and data that other devices can call remotely.

Interfacing with the IoT System

When building an IoT product, personal, commercial, or industrial, an interactive user interface is usually required. Depending on the product's purpose and how it is meant to be used, the interfacing mechanism can vary significantly. While for a smart coffee machine, the system needs to be equipped with a friendly display that the user can interact with, for an industrial monitoring solution the interfacing mechanism needs to be simple, clear, and easy to use. Also, if the solution you built is designed to be integrated within a larger platform, it also needs to support an interfacing mechanism with external systems (e.g., machine-to-machine communications).

User Interface

When it comes to offering an interface from which the user can control the solution you provide, the focus falls on the user experience and depending on what kind of product you develop, and there are several interfacing options.

For commercial products that are designed for regular users, such as smart vacuum cleaners or smart lighting systems, it is important to offer an intuitive control interface. This is why the majority of such devices come with a touch screen attached.

Touchscreen

The touchscreen is usually connected directly to the edge device and displays an interface through which the user can control and monitor it. The touchscreen behaves similarly to any regular screen that you would connect to a computer to display information. It can also act as a regular mouse, transmitting the user's events such as click, long-click, drag, etc. Some of the touch displays have more complicated behavior and require drivers to be installed so the device can recognize them. In this case, the touch events are transmitted differently to the device.

In either of the cases, the devices need to be capable of running a graphical user interface (GUI). For this, you have to ensure that a display server runs on the device. The display server is an application responsible for collecting the events from input devices such as a keyboard or mouse, sending it to the operating system for processing, and finally displaying the appropriate output on the display screen. Some of the most used such servers are X11, Wayland, or Mir.

Web Application

Another more versatile user interface option is to offer a web platform that users can access from their computers, tablets, or phones.

In this case, the edge device sends and retrieves the relevant information to and from a web server. The service can be accessed by users from a browser where data coming from the IoT device is displayed, and actions are executed by users. These actions are then transmitted by the server to the edge device, controlling the product.

The main advantage, in this case, is that the users can control and monitor the IoT devices remotely. On the other hand, this makes the system functionality dependent on the Internet or a local network connection. If the connection is lost, information between the edge device and the web server cannot be exchanged. Unfortunately, this architecture also generates several security risks. All sensitive data transmitted to and from the edge device can be intercepted or altered in a malicious manner. Therefore, somebody could manipulate the device in a dangerous way or could take hold of sensitive information.

To prevent all these risks, some IoT products use the edge device to host the web server, allowing the users to access it only if they are connected to the same network. While this approach reduces the device's accessibility, it also makes it independent from an Internet connection and significantly reduces some of the security risks.

Physical Controls

For industrial platforms, the control system needs to be accessible and reliable in exchange for a less attractive interface.

While many industrial systems offer web interfaces for monitoring and control, they also provide physical control over the devices. In this case, products expose buttons and switches that enable direct control over critical components such as motors and valves. Since these mechanisms are directly connected to the machines, they ensure fast control. In addition, simple displays or even LEDs are used to signal the current status of the equipment.

Platform Interface

Many IoT solutions are designed to be modular and easy to integrate into larger infrastructures. Therefore, the functionalities supported by the product can be extended and abstracted within a larger solution. As such, the platform to be extended needs to provide a way to interact with it. There are two main approaches: libraries and REST APIs.

Libraries

The simplest, classic way to implement and expose basic general functionalities is to group them and wrap them as libraries. While this approach works very well for local operating systems and any complex software packages, for distributed environments such as the IoT, it is difficult to distribute the library among devices. This brings a lot of installation and maintenance overhead, and as such, there are very few modern solutions relying on this approach.

A possible way to extend libraries over networks is to use Remote Procedure Calls (RPC). In this way, edge devices can reliably call functions that reside on different machines over the IoT network.

REST API

Most of the software platforms built nowadays are delivered under the form of Software as a Service (SaS). In this case, the platforms offer a web interface through which users can access the solutions, but most of them also expose a representational state transfer (REST) API, which allows them to be integrated into other platforms.

In this case, the solution runs in the cloud, and the service provider is the one responsible for all the maintenance and updates. The integrator, or user, authenticates on the platform, and with the help of GET, POST, PUT, etc. calls can access the resources of the core platform. We refer to the calls exposed by the platform as its Application Program Interface (API), and if the calls are RESTful operations, we call it the REST API. Most of the time, the REST API is built using web resources. Resources are identified using their Uniform Resource Identifiers (URI), while requests and replies use HTTP (usually formatted using HTML, XML, or JSON) and can contain new hypertext links that point to new resources in the RESTful system.

The main advantage of RESTful systems is that users accessing the resources have no direct access to the underlying software platform, and therefore they do not have to bother with installing external libraries or managing the software systems. They can focus on building their own solution around the available platforms. On the other hand, if the provider changes one of the resources, the users also have to update their solutions. This is why the users need to dedicate time and effort to keep their solutions up to date with the latest changes.

Software for IoT Systems

So far, we have seen that IoT systems rely on various devices that exchange information between themselves and with the users. An important factor that enables the devices' smart behavior is the software that runs on them.

Software Characteristics

Many of the characteristics of commercial and industrial IoT products are reflected in the applications that the devices run. The applications need to be carefully designed to meet the general requirements of any IoT system, with an emphasis on reliability and security.

Based on the main attributes of IoT solutions, we can identify the following aspects that need to be taken into account when building applications that run on the Raspberry Pi or other edge devices:

- Resource consumption – If we did not emphasize this enough, we mention once again that devices integrated into IoT solutions have reduced capabilities and usually rely on a constrained energy source, such as a battery. Because of this, it is very important to ensure that the software that runs on the devices does not waste their resources. In this regard, we should make sure that we do the minimum required number of computations to achieve the expected results and that any operation that the CPU has to execute has a well-defined purpose and is done as efficiently as possible.

- Real time – For industrial solutions, real-time response is crucial. This means that for certain cases, the software we build has to process input data as fast as possible and employ an efficient response to the trigger.

- Stability – To ensure the systems we deploy are robust and stable, we need to make sure that the software running on them handles all exceptions and corner cases and does not crash at any time. For this reason, the testing phase is crucial. During this step, all events need to be thoroughly replicated and observed how the software behaves in every possible condition. Software and hardware *watchdog timers* are used to automatically reset or shut down temporarily the devices that are unresponsive in remote places. By shutting down systems, we can also mitigate against some DDoS attacks.

- Modularity – Since heterogeneity is an important characteristic of IoT systems, the applications need to be developed based on components that are easy to extend and modify. We need to be able to easily integrate a new hardware or software component to the original system while preserving its main characteristics.

- Scalability – We need to keep in mind that IoT systems need to run on and handle thousands of simultaneous sensors and devices that exchange data between each other.

- Security – Both commercial and industrial IoT
  solutions handle sensitive data and control
  mechanisms. This is why security is imperative when
  building any IoT application.

Software Development

Developing applications for IoT systems is different from building other
software products such as desktop, mobile or web applications. This is
mainly due to the components and specific purposes of IoT systems.

First of all, the software in controlling an IoT system depends greatly
on the hardware characteristics of the system. While for a smart coffee
machine we are less interested in the power consumption, for a remote
farm monitoring solution, we aim to reduce the processing to increase
the battery lifetime. In a similar manner, when we talk about building
industrial systems, the most important aspect is how responsive the
platform is, while for consumer applications, we might dedicate more
resources to develop a friendly user experience to the detriment of fast
response times. This can impact the way we develop our applications, as
each instruction we call has an impact on the battery life or the response
time. Most of the time, most IoT systems have to balance among various
key performance indicators.

Secondly, in many of these systems, the user interface might be
nonexisting. Most of the time, applications are developed for a device
(Raspberry Pi or similar) that has no keyboard, mouse, or screen. In
this case, device access and control are an important aspect that the
developers have to tackle.

Considering these challenges and characteristics, private companies
and the open source community have built development tools specially
designed for IoT development and prototyping. These tools consist of both
advanced programming environments, but also programming languages
specific to IoT applications.

Programming Languages

When talking about software development for embedded devices programming, most of the people think about C as the main programming language. However, there are a plethora of other popular choices, depending on what kind of IoT application you aim to build.

First of all, any complete, commercial/industrial IoT system will consist of various sensors and actuators that communicate with a central unit. Many of these peripherals are complex devices that implement communication protocols. These peripherals usually contain a microcontroller that needs to be programmed. For these, at the moment, C is the most suitable programming language. While there are also lightweight interpreters that enable JavaScript or Python to be used for microcontroller programming (JerryScript[22] and MicroPython[23]), most devices of this kind support only C programming.

Secondly, the local processing and storage devices (Raspberry Pi or similar) used in IoT systems are programmed to communicate with the peripherals on the one hand, and with the cloud, on the other hand. Therefore, programming these devices requires handling network connections, file manipulation, and other similar operations. Usually, using C for these applications brings a large overhead in the development time and makes them more prone to development bugs. In this case, languages such as Python or JavaScript are widely used. There are also other alternatives, among which Java and C++ are particularly popular.[24]

Furthermore, for an edge device that is also connected to a display, we need to use a programming language that supports building user interfaces. In this case, the most popular choices are either building Java or

---

[22]https://jerryscript.net/

[23]https://micropython.org/

[24]https://dzone.com/articles/how-to-choose-the-best-programming-language-for-io

Python applications that integrate User Interface (UI) libraries or building a web application that runs on the device. In this case, technologies such as HTML, CSS, and JavaScript are used.

Besides the classical programming languages, IoT systems can also be designed and modeled using visual programming environments. This approach is especially suitable for industrial systems, where we design applications as complex pipelines that transfer and process data.

The most popular visual programming interface for IIoT systems is Laboratory Virtual Instrument Engineering Workbench (LabVIEW).[25] This is an industrial development environment designed by National Instruments. Another visual programming environment, which is widely used for both industry and prototyping, is Node-RED,[26] developed by IBM. Both platforms enable the creation of flow diagrams, where each element is a function that receives data from the previous connection, processes it, and sends the result further on.

For industrial applications that also require a user interface, systems such as Crank[27] or Qt[28] enable fast development of UI screens by dragging and dropping elements such as buttons, labels, boxes, etc.

Development Environments

IoT application development can be divided into two main phases: prototyping and scale production, each having specific challenges. Thus, we can use various development environments, each optimized for one of these phases.

IoT prototyping should be a fast process. In this case, the main challenge is the difficult hardware setup process. For example, in case

---

[25]www.ni.com/ro-ro/shop/labview.html

[26]https://nodered.org/

[27]www.cranksoftware.com/

[28]www.qt.io/

the application we aim to build should run on a Raspberry Pi, we need to configure the device and find a way to upload the application on it. We can use a screen and a keyboard to program devices that run a complete operating system with UI integrated. However, in most cases, we have the device encased, connected to various sensors and actuators. In this case, we need a way to program it remotely.

To this end, many Integrated Development Environments (IDEs) support various plug-ins that allow you to establish a connection to the device and program it remotely. However, there are also some IDEs especially designed to enable the programming of an embedded device without the need to connect to it directly. Two examples are JetBrains[29] and Wyliodrin STUDIO.[30]

As Wyliodrin STUDIO is open source, does not require any account signup, and has no costs attached, this is the IDE that we will use to build the applications in the following chapters.

Shifting from IoT prototyping to large-scale production poses a lot of diverse challenges. First, once the application for an IoT platform has been developed, it needs to be deployed on all hardware (currently produced and already in production). In general, this is a complex process that requires all devices to be flashed with the same software.

Another important aspect is pushing application updates. Similar to other software applications, IoT systems require periodic updates for both new features and security reasons. As the system rarely comes with a user interface, updates need to be done remotely and to ensure there are no failures along the process. However, software failures are imminent when talking about any devices. While we aim to reduce the number of failures, we can never prevent them completely. Diagnosing a production device that has no user interface is another challenge. This requires a specialized way to monitor and control it remotely.

---

[29]www.jetbrains.com/

[30]https://wyliodrin.studio/

Considering all these challenges, companies have developed solutions meant to handle IoT software development, management and deployment. These solutions enable producers to remotely deploy software on the devices while allowing them to monitor and control the deployed products in real-time.

Examples of such IoT industrial development and management solutions are IoTWay,[31] Balena,[32] or Mender.[33] These applications use container technologies to package the applications and publish them to a large number of IoT devices. They also enable developers to monitor and diagnose devices and publish application updates, if necessary.

Wyliodrin STUDIO

In this book, we will guide you through prototyping applications that can be easily turned into commercial or industrial IoT systems. As a result, we need a programming environment designed for IoT prototyping. This is why we choose to use Wyliodrin STUDIO.

Wyliodrin STUDIO is an open source, web-based IDE for IoT development. The platform comes in two flavors: a local version that can be installed on any platform or a browser version. The IDE is compatible with various embedded devices (Raspberry Pi, NXP Rapid IoT Prototyping Kit, UDOO, and BeagleBone Black), and it enables developers to control and deploy applications on the devices remotely. The applications can be written in Python or JavaScript, while bash scripts can also be created and executed. In addition, a visual programming language, based on Google Blockly, is also supported.

---

[31]https://iotway.io/
[32]www.balena.io/
[33]https://mender.io/

In Chapter 2, we will provide a full overview of Wyliodrin STUDIO and how to use it to program the Raspberry Pi.

Summary

In this chapter, we provided an outline of general Internet of Things systems, which we illustrated as the IoT stack. We then outlined the differences between prototyping, commercial, and industrial solutions with an emphasis on the special characteristics of the solutions implemented at the industrial scale. While for prototyping purposes, scalability and reliability are not crucial factors to be taken into account, for commercial and especially industrial solutions scaling the solution is a problem in itself.

As the following chapters of this book will focus on how to build commercial and industrial systems using the Raspberry Pi, we reviewed some hardware and software solutions that enable us to integrate the Pi into industrial systems. Another aspect that we presented in this introductory chapter consists of the main communication protocols used for data transmission between sensors and devices, and between devices. In the next chapters, we will use many of these in our applications. We then discussed ways in which we can enable users to interact with our IoT applications or, better yet, how to build applications that can be integrated into larger systems.

Finally, we also mentioned some of the challenges faced when building applications for the IoT devices and presented Wyliodrin STUDIO, the platform that we will use in the following chapters to help us overcome these concerns.

In the following chapters, we will deal with all these aspects in a more detailed and concrete approach by integrating the presented technologies into real-life applications.

Further Reading

The purpose of this chapter was to provide an overview of IoT systems, without going into the details of any particular technology. As such, the purpose of this section is to provide further reading directions for most of the technologies discussed in this chapter and which will also be used subsequently in the book.

Several books outlining the basics of the IoT have been very well received by the readers. For a technical description that covers terminology, principles, and solutions for the IoT, we highlight books by Timothy Chou,[34] Maciej Kranz,[35] and Perry Lea.[36] For a commercial/business approach to IoT solutions, we recommend Bruce Sinclair's book.[37] For those interested in the history of SCADA systems, we recommend the description given by Jerry Russell.[38] We also highlight several video resources that provide general overviews of IoT technologies such as Harvard's CS50 class given by James Whittaker,[39] Benson Hougland's TEDx talk[40] on the IoT, and Alexandru Radovici's introductory IoT lecture.[41]

---

[34]www.amazon.com/Precision-Principles-Practices-Solutions-Internet/dp/1329843568/

[35]www.amazon.com/Building-Internet-Things-Implement-Competitors-ebook/dp/B01MXJ3QO9

[36]www.amazon.com/Internet-Things-Architects-communication-infrastructure/dp/1788470591

[37]www.amazon.com/IoT-Inc-Company-Internet-Outcome-ebook/dp/B071DZZRQS

[38]web.archive.org/web/20150811051350/http://scadahistory.com/

[39]www.youtube.com/watch?v=ci4kbCmEmOI

[40]www.youtube.com/watch?v=_AlcRoqS65E

[41]www.youtube.com/watch?v=G4-CtKkrOmc

Furthermore, there are many excellent resources in the literature that focus and detail a particular aspect of the IoT. We provide several reading materials, and we discuss hardware, software, and communications protocols for the IoT separately. We conclude the reading list with a few specialized IoT topics.

The hardware tool we will use throughout this book is the Raspberry Pi. Aside from the resources and tutorials[42] on the official web site of the Raspberry Pi Foundation, we can recommend the following books by Sean McManus[43] and Simon Monk.[44] Several very good video resources also include the introduction to the Raspberry Pi by sentdex[45] or the very detailed coverage by Paul McWhorter.[46]

In this book, to develop the software components we will mainly use the JavaScript programming language (Node.js). More broadly, to review the web programming concepts, we recommend the book by Julie C. Meloni and Jennifer Kyrnin,[47] Edureka!'s video tutorial introduction,[48] and the detailed video tutorial by Full Stack Web Development.[49]

---

[42]www.wiley.com/en-it/Raspberry+Pi+User+Guide-p-9781118464496

[43]www.amazon.com/Raspberry-Pi-Dummies-Computers/dp/1119412005

[44]www.amazon.com/Raspberry-Pi-Cookbook-Software-Solutions/dp/1491939109

[45]www.youtube.com/playlist?list=PLQVvvaaOQuDesV8WWHLLXW_avmTzHmJLv

[46]www.youtube.com/playlist?list=PLGsOVKk2DiYypuwUUM2wxzcI9BJHK4Bfh

[47]www.amazon.com/HTML-JavaScript-Sams-Teach-Yourself/dp/0672338084/

[48]www.youtube.com/watch?v=Q33KBiDriJY

[49]www.youtube.com/playlist?list=PLwoh6bBAszPrES-EOajos_E9gvRbL27wz

For Node.js specifically, we suggest Mario Casciaro and Luciano Mammino's book,[50] and the video tutorial by the Free Code Camp.[51] For useful Node.js code snippets, we recommend the Node.js Notes for Professionals.[52]

Throughout this chapter, we assume a general knowledge of networking concepts and communication protocols. To overview computer networks, an excellent reference is the book by Andrew S. Tanenbaum[53] and Geek's Lesson's video lecture.[54] For industrial technologies, in particular, we recommend David Hanes' comprehensive book[55] and the introduction to IoT communication protocols by Antonio Almeida and Jaime González-Arintero Berciano.[56]

Specialized IoT topics include Sravani Bhattacharjee's securing IoT devices and networks,[57] the book on artificial intelligence and big data for IoT[58] by Robert Stackowiak and coauthors, the book on 5G and IoT technologies[59] by Yulei Wu and coauthors, and the book on blockchain technologies applied to IoT systems[60] by Liehuang Zhu and coauthors.

---

[50]www.amazon.com/Node-js-Design-Patterns-server-side-applications/dp/1785885588

[51]www.youtube.com/watch?v=RLtyhwFtXQA

[52]https://books.goalkicker.com/NodeJSBook/

[53]www.amazon.com/Computer-Networks-Andrew-S-Tanenbaum-ebook/dp/B006Y1BKGC

[54]www.youtube.com/watch?v=QKfk7YFILws

[55]www.amazon.co.uk/IoT-Fundamentals-Networking-Technologies-Protocols/dp/1587144565

[56]www.youtube.com/watch?v=s6ZtfLmvQMU

[57]www.amazon.com/dp/B078MTMN77

[58]www.amazon.com/Big-Data-Internet-Things-Architecture/dp/1484209877

[59]www.amazon.com/5G-Enabled-Internet-Things-Yulei-Wu/dp/0367190109

[60]www.amazon.com/Blockchain-Technology-Internet-Things-Liehuang/dp/3030217655

Finally, we also have to mention the large-scale IoT management systems developed by the largest information technology companies: AWS IoT[61] by Amazon, Google Cloud IoT[62], and Azure IoT Hub[63] by Microsoft. Other industrial companies have also developed their own platforms: Siemens' Mindsphere, Cisco's Kinetic and Jasper, IBM's Watson, GE's Predix, and Schneider Electric's EcoStruxure. While each one of these platforms has its own weaknesses, the sheer number of existing solutions highlights the growing interest in the development of IoT applications.

---

[61]docs.aws.amazon.com/whitepapers/latest/aws-overview/internet-of-things-services.html

[62]https://cloud.google.com/solutions/iot/

[63]https://azure.microsoft.com/en-us/services/iot-hub/

CHAPTER 2

Getting Started with the Raspberry Pi and Wyliodrin STUDIO

For the work outlined in this book, all IoT applications that we develop are composed of four major design components (IoT application stack):

1. **The hardware** component consists of a central computing platform which connects various physical elements: custom-made circuitry and devices, sensors, actuators, power supplies, connectivity (either Wi-Fi or network) are just a few we mention.

2. **The software** component implements all logic and action that needs to take place locally on the hardware platform and typically consists of several elements, including an operating system, initialization and diagnosis modules for the hardware components, local rules and software logic to be executed between the sensors and actuators, local data storage modules, and primitive data management (processing) modules.

© Ioana Culic; Alexandru Radovici; Cristian Rusu 2020
I. Culic et al., *Commercial and Industrial Internet of Things Applications with the Raspberry Pi*,
https://doi.org/10.1007/978-1-4842-5296-3_2

3. **The network** (connectivity) component refers to the fact that an IoT application has to communicate with the world in several ways: it has to be able to receive information and commands from an authenticated user, has to collect data and send it to more advanced storage and processing units (mostly in the cloud), and has to communicate with social media accounts or send updates and alerts about changes in its environment.

4. **The management of the IoT application** refers to the deployment and monitoring of the behavior of such a system once the application is up and running. Deployment refers to the ability of developers to set up and update the software underlying the IoT application over the Internet. Remember, we expect IoT devices to number in the billions, and therefore special care has to be given to the efficient management of these devices.

For all these components, the development process depends a lot on the design and programming environments used. Proper setup and tools can significantly reduce the development time and help rapidly complete a fully functioning prototype with ease. In many cases, most of the time spent building IoT applications is dedicated to setting up the hardware, deploying the software onto it, and then extensively test the stability and reliability of the solution. However, in the prototyping phase (concerned with the development of the first three aforementioned components), the goal is to get an application up and running as fast as possible and then focus separately on the long-term management of the application.

This book guides you through prototyping commercial and industrial IoT applications by following the development of the four components enumerated in the list. Therefore, at this stage, we focus on building the application and performing the hardware setup, which can then be perfected to an actual product. In this context, the hardware and software tools we choose to use are specially designed to be fast as they are dedicated to prototyping. In the following chapters, we will use a Raspberry Pi as the primary hardware device, which we will program and control from the Wyliodrin STUDIO programming environment.

In this chapter, we help you get started with using the Raspberry Pi and Wyliodrin STUDIO. Finally, we launch a simple Hello World application on the device.

About the Raspberry Pi

The Raspberry Pi is a pocket-sized computer with powerful capabilities. It was first released by the Raspberry Pi Foundation in 2012 to be an affordable and easy-to-use educational device for teaching programming. Since 2012, several versions of the Raspberry Pi have been released, with improved capabilities. There are three form factors: Zero, A, and B.

The Raspberry Pi Zero is the smallest and less powerful one and is provided in two versions, Zero and Zero W (there is also a Zero WH version, which is the Raspberry Pi Zero W with soldered header). It has an ARMv6 CPU, 512 MB of memory, and one micro USB port. The Zero W version adds Wi-Fi. Both versions have a special Raspberry Pi camera socket.

As of 2019, the latest Raspberry Pi Model B, V4, has an ARMv8[1] 1.5 GHz processor, onboard wireless and BLE, 2 USB ports, 2 USB 3 ports, an Ethernet port, and two micro HDMI connectors (Figure 2-1). In addition, it also has a special connector for a camera module and one for touchscreen connection. It is powered using a USB-C cable.

The Raspberry Pi Model A is similar to model B, except that it has only one USB port and no Ethernet adapter.

For industrial applications, the Raspberry Pi Foundation provides the Compute Module. The form factor is that of a laptop RAM memory board. Users are expected to build a mainboard that is able to accommodate this module. As this is a little difficult to use out of the box, we do not focus on this model throughout this book. It is important to keep in mind that any project working on one of the Raspberry Pi models could be trivially extended to the Compute Module.

Besides the characteristics specific to any computer, the Raspberry Pi also exposes various pins that can be connected to peripherals such as sensors and actuators, making it easy to integrate into any IoT application. When it comes to the pins exposed by the device, we have the following types: GPIO, 3.3V, 5V, GND, PWM (software), SPI, I2C, and UART serial.

---

[1]The software provided for the Raspberry Pi (Raspbian) is built for ARMv7, thus the Raspberry Pi is considered an ARMv7 when talking about the software for it.

Figure 2-1. *Raspberry Pi version 4[2]*

The Raspberry Pi also has an SD card slot, as the SD card is usually the only available storage for the device, similar to the hard drive in computers. The SD card is the place where all the data is stored, including the operating system. As the Raspberry Pi has USB connectors, one may connect additional storage devices. Newer models are even able to boot operating systems (OS) from a USB storage. Older models though are only able to boot from the SD card.

Similarly to any other computer, the Raspberry Pi also runs an operating system. While there are various operating systems and distributions available for it, in this book we will use Raspbian, a Debian distribution that the Raspberry Pi Foundation maintains and provides on their web site.

---

[2]www.amazon.com/Raspberry-Model-2019-Quad-Bluetooth/dp/B07TD42S27

Due to its endurance and low price, the Raspberry Pi has become widely popular as a prototyping and educational device and since the release of the Compute Module, it has also been integrated into various commercial and industrial applications. As of 2018, its sales reached more than 19 million units.

Due to its characteristics and popularity, we have chosen the Raspberry Pi as the main hardware platform for building the products we will describe later in the book.

Note   The specific device we use for all the examples is a Raspberry Pi 4. However, you can choose to work with any of the versions.

About Wyliodrin STUDIO

Wyliodrin STUDIO is an integrated development environment designed for prototyping IoT applications. It is a web-based application that is used through a browser or by downloading and launching it locally.

Wyliodrin STUDIO supports various embedded devices such as the Raspberry Pi, BeagleBone Black, NXP Rapid IoT Prototyping Kit, and others, which can be programmed, controlled, and monitored through the platform. As an IoT application management tool, Wyliodrin STUDIO fits into the fourth category of the IoT application stack described.

Wyliodrin STUDIO is easy to install, and hardware devices can be easily connected to it, without much additional configuration required. Moreover, all the programs developed are stored locally, not on the Raspberry Pi, which enables the users to share and deploy them on multiple devices at once easily. These advantages are also the reasons why we choose to use Wyliodrin STUDIO as the primary programming environment for our applications.

Wyliodrin STUDIO comes in two varieties: a local version that needs to be downloaded and runs on your computer and a web version that can be accessed from the browser. Both versions have a similar interface and can be used to program and control the Raspberry Pi or other supported devices. Both versions are designed to store the projects and other information about the device on the local computer.

The main advantage of the web version is that it does not have to be installed on a specific computer. Thus, you can access it from anywhere and have control over your devices. Also, any platform updates are visible with a simple refresh of the page, while for the local version updating the application requires to re-download it. The downside is that it is dependent on an Internet connection, whereas the local version can be accessed only from your computer, but a local connection is enough to get you running. The web version also implies a couple of extra steps in the setup process, but it allows you to program and control the Raspberry Pi without a physical connection to it. The local version works only if the Raspberry Pi is in the same network as the computer where Wyliodrin STUDIO is running.

Note   The browser version of Wyliodrin STUDIO stores projects locally in the browser. This means that two different browsers on the same computer will generate two different local storages. Sharing projects directly between browsers is currently not possible.

Tip   If you have an Internet connection accessible for the Raspberry Pi, we recommend using the web version of the Wyliodrin STUDIO as it is easier to keep up to date with the latest platform changes.

The first step in programming your Raspberry Pi is to install the Wyliodrin STUDIO IDE and connect the device to the platform.

Run Wyliodrin STUDIO

To get started with Wyliodrin STUDIO, we first need to access the following web site: *https://wyliodrin.studio*. Here we have two options: download the local version or access the web version. Depending on the solution that we aim to use, we have to choose one of the two.

Run Wyliodrin STUDIO Locally

In this case, we have the possibility to download an executable that runs on the computer, with no dependency on an Internet connection. For this to happen, we hit the download button and wait for the executable to be downloaded. Once the download is complete, depending on the computer's operating system, you have to either launch the executable or install the application to get running.

For Windows platforms, it is enough to launch the downloaded executable and the installer starts automatically. When the process is complete, Wyliodrin STUDIO can be launched from the taskbar.

For Linux-based platforms an *AppImage* file is downloaded. By double-clicking the file, the application is launched.

For macOS systems, the downloaded file is of *dmg* type. By double-clicking it you launch a pop-up that asks you to move the executable to the **Applications** folder.

Note   As the application is not downloaded from the AppStore, to open it for the first time, you might have to right-click the application icon and select *open*. Then, a pop-up appears. After you select *open* again, the application launches.

Run Wyliodrin STUDIO in the Browser

The second option is running Wyliodrin STUDIO directly in the browser. In this case, you simply need to hit the *Use Wyliodrin STUDIO in the browser* button and an instance of the application is launched.

Note   The main difference between the local and the web versions of Wyliodrin STUDIO is the install process. Both versions store the data on the local computer.

Connect the Raspberry Pi to Wyliodrin STUDIO

Now that we have the IDE in place, the next step is to connect the Raspberry Pi so we can control it and deploy applications onto it.

The main requirement, in this case, is to have a Raspberry Pi that can be connected either to the Internet or the local network and an SD card to store the operating system.

Note   If you have a Raspberry Pi that is already running a Raspbian image, you can skip to the "Manual Setup" section, which guides you through the configuration process required to register the device to Wyliodrin STUDIO.

As we already mentioned, the Raspberry Pi runs the operating system from the SD card, so we first need to download the SD card image and write it on the card. Since we are using Wyliodrin STUDIO, we do not download the Raspbian image from the official web site, but we download the SD card image that Wyliodrin STUDIO supports. This is the standard Raspbian Lite distribution on top of which some scripts were configured to run, enabling the Raspberry Pi to communicate with Wyliodrin STUDIO.

Tip   To write the image on the SD card you have to connect it to your computer. If your computer or laptop does not have an SD card slot, you need a USB adaptor in order to do this.

To download the image, we have to access the following web site: https://wyliodrinstudio.readthedocs.io and select *Board Setup*. Here we find a link that starts the download of the SD card image. Once this is done, we need to unzip the file to obtain the SD card image. The next step is to write it on the SD card. For this, we can choose among various applications. We recommend using Etcher.

To download Etcher, we go to www.balena.io/etcher and hit the download button (Figure 2-2). Once the download is done, we can launch Etcher.

Figure 2-2. *Download Etcher*

Finally, we have to insert the SD card into the computer, select the image file and the SD card as a source, and hit the *Flash* button (Figure 2-3).

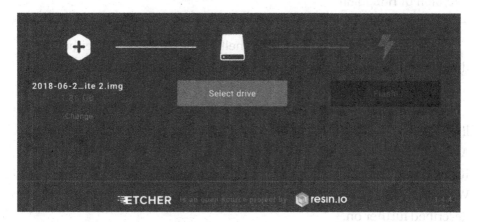

Figure 2-3. The flashing process

Caution   Please be very careful when selecting the destination disk as selecting a wrong one might risk erasing the data on your computer.

Now that the SD card contains the Wyliodrin STUDIO image, you simply need to insert it into the Raspberry Pi, connect the device to the network, and power it on.

Tip   We recommend using an Ethernet connection for the Raspberry Pi. If you wish to use a Wi-Fi connection, you have to enable the SSH and set it manually via a terminal.

Manual Setup

In case you have previously configured your Raspberry Pi, you might not want to re-flash the SD card to keep specific configurations. In this case, you can run a set of commands that install the necessary tools on the device so you can connect it to Wyliodrin STUDIO.

Note   We are assuming here that your Raspberry Pi is running a version of Raspbian.

To get started we need to open a shell on the Raspberry Pi, either by directly controlling the device or via SSH. All the configurations are done in the Raspberry Pi shell.

The commands to be used are thoroughly described at the following link: `https://wyliodrinstudio.readthedocs.io` (select Board Setup). After you finish following the tutorial on the web site, by rebooting the Raspberry Pi you can connect it to Wyliodrin STUDIO. Based on the Wyliodrin STUDIO version that you decided to use, the following steps are described further on.

Tip   The download image depends on the Raspberry Pi version you use.

Connect the Raspberry Pi to the Local Version of Wyliodrin STUDIO

If you are using the local version of Wyliodrin STUDIO, once you connect the Raspberry Pi to the network, the device appears in the device list. You need to hit the *Connect* button and a pop-up displaying the available devices appear. To connect the device to Wyliodrin STUDIO we have to select the desired Raspberry Pi and insert the required credentials (Figure 2-4). This information is necessary as the local version of Wyliodrin STUDIO uses the SSH protocol to communicate with the device. The result is that any operation you do on the platform behaves as you would do it directly on the device.

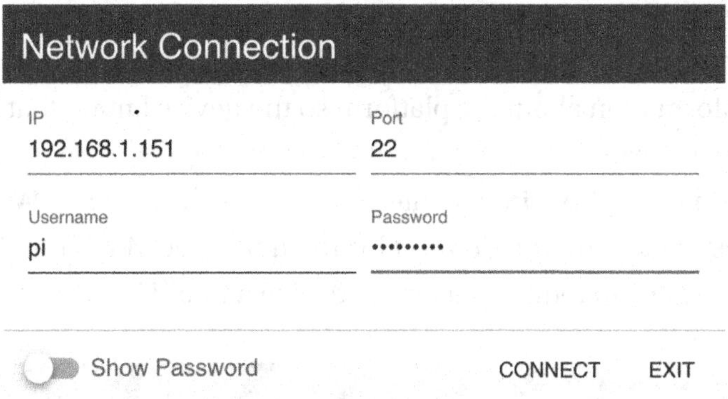

Network Connection

IP
192.168.1.151

Port
22

Username
pi

Password
•••••••••

Show Password   CONNECT   EXIT

Figure 2-4. Connect to Raspberry Pi

Note   The default credentials for the Raspbian image you downloaded are username: pi and password: raspberry.

When you connect to the device, the platform suggests that you change the default password (Figure 2-5). To do this, you need to open the SHELL tab, press any key to get it started, and run the `passwd` command. This is important for security reasons and it prevents others to gain control over your Pi.

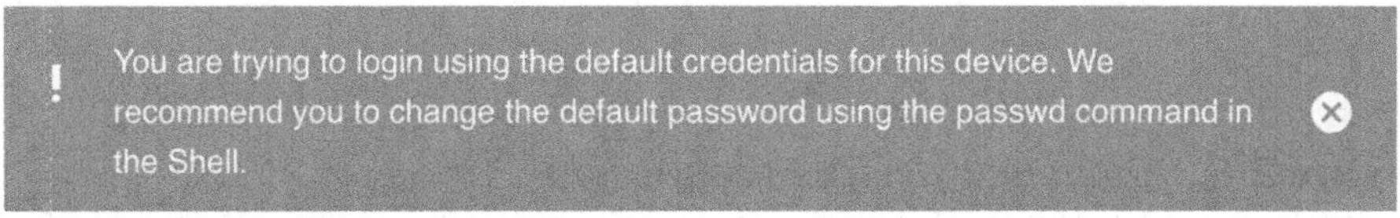

You are trying to login using the default credentials for this device. We recommend you to change the default password using the passwd command in the Shell.

Figure 2-5. Change credentials suggestion

Connect the Raspberry Pi to Browser Version of Wyliodrin STUDIO

To connect the Raspberry Pi to the web version of Wyliodrin STUDIO, an Internet connection is required. Also, to enable the communication between the IDE and the device, a configuration file, called **wyliodrin.json,** needs to be stored on the SD card. This file contains information identifying the device so that it is recognized by the platform, but also contains information about the platform so the device knows that it is communicating with.

To obtain the **wyliodrin.json** file, inside the web version of Wyliodrin STUDIO we need to hit the *Connect* button and select *Add Web device*. This shows a pop-up requesting for the device name (Figure 2-6).

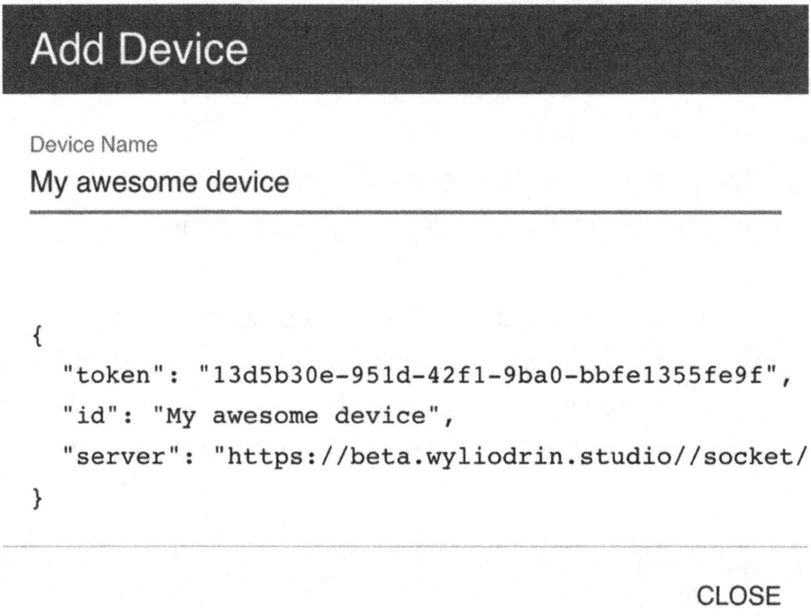

Add Device

Device Name
My awesome device

```
{
    "token": "13d5b30e-951d-42f1-9ba0-bbfe1355fe9f",
    "id": "My awesome device",
    "server": "https://beta.wyliodrin.studio//socket/
}
```

CLOSE

Figure 2-6. *Add a new device to connect to*

As we insert the necessary information a JSON structure is generated based on this. The structure contains the following information:

- server – The endpoint with which the device communicates.

- id – The name of the device; this can be changed to any string you prefer.

- token – The unique identifier of the device; it is automatically generated by the Wyliodrin STUDIO to identify the user and should never be changed.

The generated JSON needs to be copied into a file called **wyliodrin.json**, and then the file needs to be placed on the SD card in the **boot** partition. To achieve this, we need to insert the flashed SD card into the computer and the partition opens automatically. We copy the file there and the card is ready to be inserted into the Raspberry Pi (Figure 2-7).

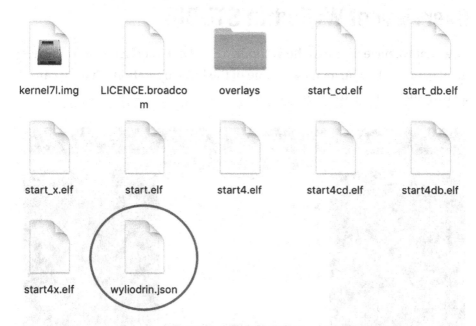

kernel7l.img	LICENCE.broadcom	overlays	start_cd.elf	start_db.elf
start_x.elf	start.elf	start4.elf	start4cd.elf	start4db.elf
start4x.elf	wyliodrin.json			

Figure 2-7. *wyliodrin.json file stored on the boot partition*

Once the file is on the SD card, we can insert the card in the Raspberry Pi, connect it to the Internet, and power it on. The final step is to select again the *Connect* button from the Wyliodrin STUDIO platform and the Raspberry Pi should appear in the devices list (Figure 2-8). By selecting the device, you initialize the connection to the platform.

Figure 2-8. *Available devices list*

Overview of Wyliodrin STUDIO

Now that we have installed the Wyliodrin STUDIO interface and connected the Raspberry Pi to it, let us see some of the basic operations that we can do with the Pi using the IDE.

Figure 2-9. *Wyliodrin STUDIO interface*

First, we have the top bar that enables us to do some basic operations such as:

- Projects Library – Launches a pop-up that allows us to create or import applications and to open the ones already available.

- Task Manager – Visualize the processes running on the Raspberry Pi and stop any of them with a press of a button. See Figure 2-9.

- Package Manager – View, add, and remove Python or Node.js packages in a visual manner.

- Network Manager – Connect the device to a different network; it is especially useful for connecting the Raspberry Pi to a Wi-Fi network without the need to use shell commands.

- Disconnect – Disconnects, reboots, or powers off the connected device.

Caution   Modifying network settings might disconnect your Raspberry Pi from the network and from Wyliodrin STUDIO. Please act carefully.

Further on, once we open a new project, we can access the five tabs available:

- Application – The tab where we write the actual source code of the application; depending on the chosen programming language, this can be similar to a text editor or it can support a visual programming interface based on blocks and other elements.

- Dashboard – This tab is designed for easy and fast debugging of IoT systems based on visual graphs such as sliders, lines, speedometers, or thermometers. The dashboard plots data coming from the running application to help us better visualize the values coming from the sensors; however, the dashboard does not store the data it receives, showing only instant values.

- Notebook – Used for prototyping and documenting the application, it allows developers to write the documentation for the application they are building while also trying out snippets of code. The code snippets can be integrated in the documentation and can be run on the connected device by pressing one button.

- Pin Layout – Displays the pins and their numbering for the device connected to the Wyliodrin STUDIO platform.

- Shell – Enables us to open a direct terminal into the device, which gives us full control over the Raspberry Pi and enables us to carry out advanced operations, such as installing new libraries.

Other configuration can be done via the menu located on the top-left side of the Wyliodrin STUDIO platform. There we can use a resistor calculator, which helps us compute the resistance based on the colors or helps us identify the resistor we need. Also, we can set the IDE into advanced or simple mode. In the simple mode, we can write one-file applications that get deployed on the device, while in advanced mode we can create directories and multiple files to build complex applications. In our case, as in the next chapters we build complex applications, we use the advanced mode of the editor.

Deploy Applications on the Raspberry Pi

Now that we are familiar with the interface and how to control the Raspberry Pi using Wyliodrin STUDIO, let us write our first application and deploy it on the device. Since in the next chapters we will use JavaScript as the main programming language, we write a simple Node.js application that displays a text in the console and then we import an external library to make an LED blink.

First, we need to create a new JavaScript application (Figure 2-10). Once the application is created, we open it and we already have the first line writing a text in the console generated.

Caution   When you try to create a new project in the browser version, you are asked to enable the persistent storage. This is required so the browser can store all your projects, otherwise you risk having projects deleted randomly. Some browsers might not support the persistent storage option enabled, in this case we recommend using a different browser or downloading your projects periodically.

To deploy the application on the device, we simply need to press the *Run* button and we see the output in the console (Figure 2-11).

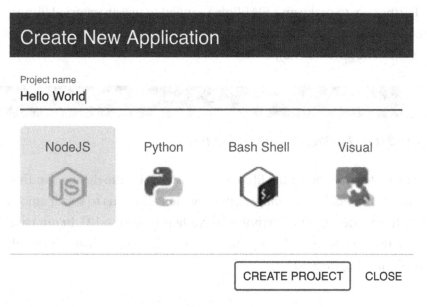

Figure 2-10. Create a new application

Figure 2-11. *Hello World application output*

Further on, to make an LED blink, we need to use an external library for controlling the Raspberry Pi pins. For JavaScript, one of the most used pin-control libraries is *onoff.*

Figure 2-12. *Package manager location*

The first step in using the library is to install it on the device. For this, we can use the *Package Manager* option which allows us to select among available libraries for both Python and Node.js (Figure 2-12). In our case, after we hit the *Package Manager* button, we select Node.js and install the *onoff* library (Figure 2-13).

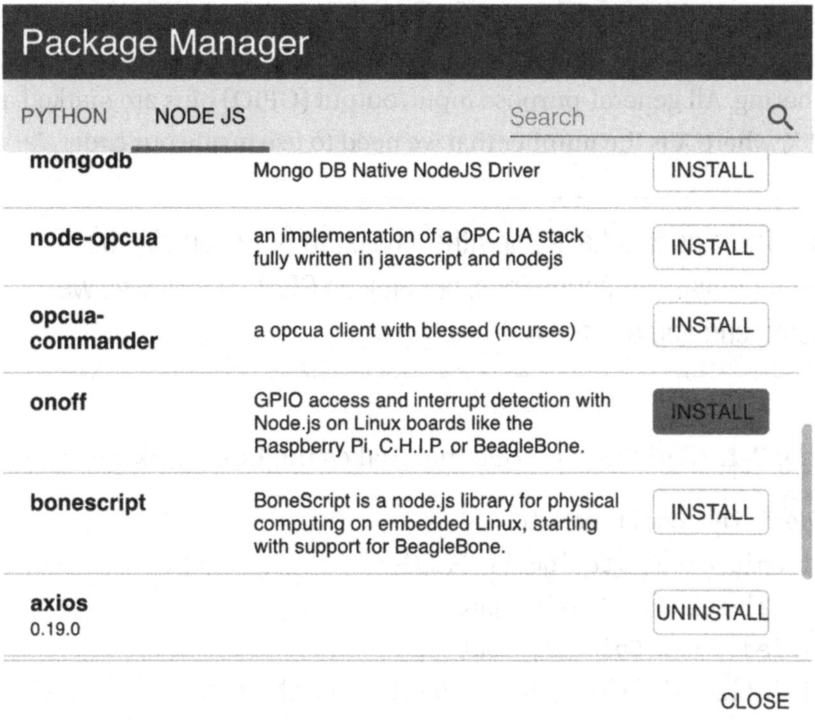

Figure 2-13. *Install the onoff library*

Note   This installs the library globally. While this is not the recommended approach for a production application, it works very well for prototyping purposes, allowing for fast development.

As we assured that the required library is installed on the system, in the **main.js** file we have imported the *onoff* module and then initialized pin 17 as output. Using the setInterval() function we used a one-second delay to write 1 or 0 on the pin, leading to the LED blinking. See Listing 2-1 for the full source code.

To choose the pins that we aim to connect the LED on, we can open the *PIN LAYOUT* tab and we see a schematic of the pins and their numbering. All general-purpose input/output (GPIO) pins are marked as *BCM X,* where *X* is the number that we need to use inside our code.

Tip The pins that have parenthesis next to BCM can also be used for advanced peripherals, not only as GPIO. This is why we recommend you use the GPIO-only pins.

Listing 2-1. The Node.js code that makes the LED blink

```
//import the onoff module
const Gpio = require('onoff').Gpio;
//initialize pin 17 as output
const led = new Gpio(17, 'out');
//initialize the value to be written on the pin
let value = 0;

console.log('Hello from JavaScript');

//call a function every 1000 milliseconds
setInterval (function (){
    //write the value on the pin
    led.writeSync(value);
    //change value from 0 to 1 and vice versa
    value = 1-value;
}, 1000);
```

After pressing the *Run* button, we should see the LED connected on pin GPIO 17 blinking.

Summary

In this chapter we went through the steps necessary to get started with developing simple IoT applications. As in the next chapters we will focus on the prototyping phase of building commercial and industrial systems, we choose the Raspberry Pi as the hardware platform and Wyliodrin STUDIO as the management interface.

The Raspberry Pi is one of the most popular hardware platforms used in education and for prototyping purposes. For further reading, we recommend browsing through the web site `www.raspberrypi.org/` to explore the various Raspberry Pi devices available on the market.

Wyliodrin STUDIO is an open source, web-based IDE for fast prototyping of IoT applications. The platform comes in two varieties: a local version and a web version and is easy to use for both beginners and advanced developers. Also, as it is open source, it can be extended and integrated into other applications. For more information on the platform, we recommend visiting the official web site `https://wyliodrin.studio`.

After the setup process is done and the Raspberry Pi is successfully connected to the Wyliodrin STUDIO platform, we can easily install packages, control the device via a shell, and most importantly deploy applications.

In the next chapters we deal with the development of the three main components of an IoT application (hardware, software, and network) and use Wyliodrin STUDIO as the deployment and management tool for the application.

CHAPTER 3

Smart Digital Signage System

In this chapter, we will go through the steps necessary to prototype a digital signage system that is connected to the Internet so you can remotely update the content it displays.

The ability of governments and businesses to mass-share information is of paramount importance. This is why cities are populated with billboards and digital panels consisting of connected screens that display dynamic commercials, timetables, environmental variables (e.g., pollution level), traffic information (such as accidents or roadblocks), or other informative materials.

A classic example of large-scale smart digital signage is Times Square in New York City, which is decorated from top to bottom with billboards and advertisements, among which the most iconic are the seven-story high NASDAQ sign (from 2000) and the Coca-Cola and Samsung advertisements (both from 2017). There are also recent changes, as work is underway to finalize the development of 20 Times Square, which will host a 1.672 square meter (or 18.000 square foot) screen made up of 16 million LEDs. Other worldwide examples include the Shibuya Crossing in Shibuya City, Tokyo, Japan; the COEX (convention, exhibition, and shopping complex) and World Trade Center area in Seoul, South Korea; or the Piccadilly Circus area in London, UK.

© Ioana Culic; Alexandru Radovici; Cristian Rusu 2020
I. Culic et al., *Commercial and Industrial Internet of Things Applications with the Raspberry Pi*,
https://doi.org/10.1007/978-1-4842-5296-3_3

All digital signage systems are based on modern electronics and software components, and they are a particularly good example of the potential that IoT holds in real-world applications. Integrating IoT technologies into the signage systems has several specific advantages:

- Create a cost-effective system that can function correctly for prolonged time periods and where ongoing maintenance can be accomplished efficiently as diagnosis information can be sent by the system periodically to a central maintenance unit where global repair decisions can be made.

- Create a context-aware system where the information shared can be delivered in real time and dynamically adapted in time to the target public and therefore significantly improving the effectiveness of the system.

- Create an interactive system by allowing personalized content (or behavior) to be created and posted by people through their social media accounts.

- Given an interactive system, analyze though data analytics the long-term interaction between the system and its users to better understand the users and improve the system.

Necessary Components

To build the digital signage system, you will need the following components:

- Raspberry Pi connected to the Internet and to Wyliodrin STUDIO.

- Any screen that can be connected via HDMI.

If you do not have an HDMI screen, you can also use a touchscreen display. For more information on how to connect the display to the Raspberry Pi, we recommend Pi Hut's tutorial.[1]

To get started with building a new application, you need to register the Raspberry Pi in the Wyliodrin STUDIO platform. This allows us to easily run the application on the device. If you have already followed Chapter 2 in this book, you should have a Pi that is registered on this platform. Otherwise, we recommend following the tutorial in Chapter 2.

The Application Architecture

Building applications that require a user interface can be done by using various technologies and in a multitude of different ways. The main options when building a UI for the Raspberry Pi are the following libraries: GTK+, Qt, and web-based libraries. GTK+ is a reliable option that provides means of building classic windows and buttons UI and requires C programming skills.[2] Qt is by far one of the best choices, supporting animations, video acceleration, and all the modern UI elements. The downside is that it requires payment of royalties for usage on embedded devices. This is why we choose to use web technologies for this book. Even though these libraries need a little more computing power, these technologies are open and free to use and run on most of the platforms. Moreover, we can easily state that today most of the applications that we use are web based, mainly because they can be run on any architecture. The result is that web technologies are under constant development, and there is a multitude of libraries

---

[1]thepihut.com/blogs/raspberry-pi-tutorials/45295044-raspberry-pi-7-touch-screen-assembly-guide

[2]While there are some bindings for other languages like Python or Node.js, these do not cover all the libraries.

and frameworks available, which allow developers to build a complex interface. In addition, the number of developers with the knowledge to build such applications is extremely high.

As the Raspberry Pi is a pretty powerful device, we choose to build the smart signage system as a web application. Since web technologies can run on any device that is able to run a browser, the UI is runnable on most embedded devices that run Linux.

Electron

The smart signage application that we are going to build is designed just like a regular web interface, which means that we need a browser to run it. While for regular web applications, where the user has a keyboard and a mouse, launching the browser to access the application is normal, for this use case we aim to run our smart signage application so it looks like it is the only one running on the system. Imagine the users seeing the browser and the interface inside it. It is obvious that this is not the desired outcome.

Therefore, we need a way of launching a web application but without the classical browser. This is where the *Electron framework* comes in hand.

Electron is a framework that allows for web applications to be run like desktop applications. Many popular applications, which behave like native apps, are actually developed on top of Electron. Some of such applications are Visual Studio Code[3] or Slack.[4]

By using Electron, we create a simple web application and launch it as a full-screen app so users see only the information that we aim to display.

---

[3]https://code.visualstudio.com/
[4]https://slack.com/

The Application

To build a new application, we first need to access the Wyliodrin STUDIO platform and create a new JavaScript project.

As we already mentioned, the application we aim to build is a web app that runs on the device using the Electron framework. This implies that the project we just created consists of several files and directories. Therefore, the first step is to set Wyliodrin STUDIO into advanced mode (Figure 3-1) and create a new folder called **UI**. This is where all files related to the web application are stored.

Figure 3-1. *Switch to advanced mode*

To create a new folder, we have to right-click the name of the project and select the *New folder* option. Insert the desired folder name and the folder is created.

Source Code

Now that we are familiar with the structure, the next step is to build the actual application. At first, the purpose is to create an app that displays some text on the screen.

As for the beginning we aim to create a simple static interface, we generate a file called **index.html**. Here we use some standard HTML tags to print the desired text.

The next step is to launch the application. If we were to talk about a regular web app, we would have a server that would return the HTML files to be rendered by the browser. However, in our case, the browser is replaced with the electron framework, which can run a JavaScript (Node. js) application that renders the interface. Therefore, we need to create a **main.js** file which launches the UI.

The index.html File

To get started, we need to create a file called **index.html** in the **UI** directory (Listing 3-1). Here we write the text *This is my first smart billboard application!*

Listing 3-1. The HTML source code

```
<!DOCTYPE html>
<html lang="en">
  <head>
    <title>Welcome</title>
  </head>
  <body>
    <center>This is my first smart billboard application!</center>
  </body>
</html>
```

The code is basic HTML that displays some centered text.

The main.js File

Once the HTML file is created, we need to build the Node.js script that actually launches the application (Listing 3-2).

Note   The **main.js** file is a Node.js script derived from Electron's examples.

Running an Electron application requires at least two processes: the main process and a render process. The main process is responsible for handling all web pages and launching them, while the render process is specific to each web page, and it handles how the web page is displayed. Therefore, when launching Electron, we have one main process and as many rendering processes as the number of web pages that the main process will launch.

While the rendering process is related to the HTML, JavaScript, and CSS files, the main process needs to be defined in a Node.js file that is executed by the Electron framework. The main process creates and destroys browser windows and handles their properties; all the rest is done within each window by the rendering process.

Listing 3-2. The main.js file

```
const electron = require('electron');
const path = require('path');
const url = require('url');

// Module to control application life.
const app = electron.app;

// Module to create native browser window.
const BrowserWindow = electron.BrowserWindow;
```

75

```
/* Keep a global reference of the window object, if you don't,
the window will be closed automatically when the JavaScript
object is garbage collected.*/
let mainWindow;
function createWindow ()
{
    // Create the browser window.
    mainWindow = new BrowserWindow({
        height: 600,
      width: 800,
        frame: false,
        webPreferences: {
                nodeIntegration: true
        }
    });
    // and load the index.html of the app.
    mainWindow.loadURL(url.format({
        pathname: path.join(__dirname, 'UI/index.html'),
        protocol: 'file:',
        slashes: true
    }));

    // Emitted when the window is closed.
    mainWindow.on('closed', function () {
    /* Dereference the window object, usually you would store
    windows in an array if your app supports multi windows,
    this is the time when you should delete the corresponding
    element.*/
        mainWindow = null;
    });
}
app.on('ready', createWindow);
```

```
// Quit when all windows are closed.
app.on('window-all-closed', function () {
    app.quit();
});

app.on('activate', function () {
    if (mainWindow === null) {
        createWindow();
    }
});
```

Now let us break the main application apart so we can discuss the essential components and gain a better understanding of the **main.js** file.

As the main process is in charge of managing all browser windows and the overall application, this requires us to create a new window to display. To achieve this, we need to import the *Electron* module, which exports all necessary sub-modules (Listing 3-3). The modules that Electron exports and which are important to us are *app* and *BrowserWindow*. The *app* module stores all information related to the application, allowing us to control its life cycle. If you are familiar with building UI applications, you should notice a familiar pattern, where the app object generates events to which we can assign specific functions. In addition, the *BrowserWindow* module allows us to handle the creation and destruction of new browser windows within the main process.

Listing 3-3. Import and create all necessary structures

```
const electron = require('electron');
// Module to control application life.
const app = electron.app;
// Class that represents a browser window.
const BrowserWindow = electron.BrowserWindow;
```

Further on, we import other necessary modules. *path* and *url* enable us to generate the link toward the **index.html** file so the browser can open it. Next, we create a new browser window where the **index.html** file is opened. Here, we need to specify the screen's dimensions. For this, you need to check your display's characteristics and set the values accordingly. We also specified that we want to have the window frame disabled. This hides the menu bar on the top. The final property of the window element, *nodeIntegration*, allows us to run Node.js files instead of simple JavaScript. As a result, we can use functions specific to Node.js (e.g., *require()*) in the JavaScript files related to the user interface (Listing 3-4).

Listing 3-4. Create the browser window

```
const path = require('path');
const url = require('url');

// Create the browser window.
mainWindow = new BrowserWindow({
width: 1180,
        height: 800,
          frame: false,
        webPreferences: {
            nodeIntegration: true }
 });
```

Next, we generate a URL to the **main.html** file and load it inside the window (Listing 3-5).

Listing 3-5. Load the UI

```
mainWindow.loadURL(url.format({
    pathname: path.join(__dirname, 'UI/index.html'),
    protocol: 'file:',
    slashes: true
}));
```

Once we defined the *createWindow()* function and clearly specified how the new browser window should be handled, we can manage the application life cycle and generate new windows accordingly. Since the Raspberry Pi is meant to be connected to a noninteractive screen and there are no other UI applications running on it, we can consider, for now, that once the Electron framework has finished loading, we can create a new window, which remains on the screen. This is why we are only interested in the *ready* event, which is triggered when Electron has finished its initialization process: `app.on('ready', createWindow);`

Installing the Necessary Libraries

Now that all the source files are ready to be deployed, the final step consists of running the application.

First, we need to install the Electron framework (Figure 3-2). Electron comes as a Node.js package that needs to be installed globally on the device. This is where the Package Manager comes in handy. To install Electron, we need to launch the Package Manager and install it from the Node.js tab.

Note   There are ways to specify all the libraries necessary for a project; we will discuss this later. For now, we install all the libraries globally.

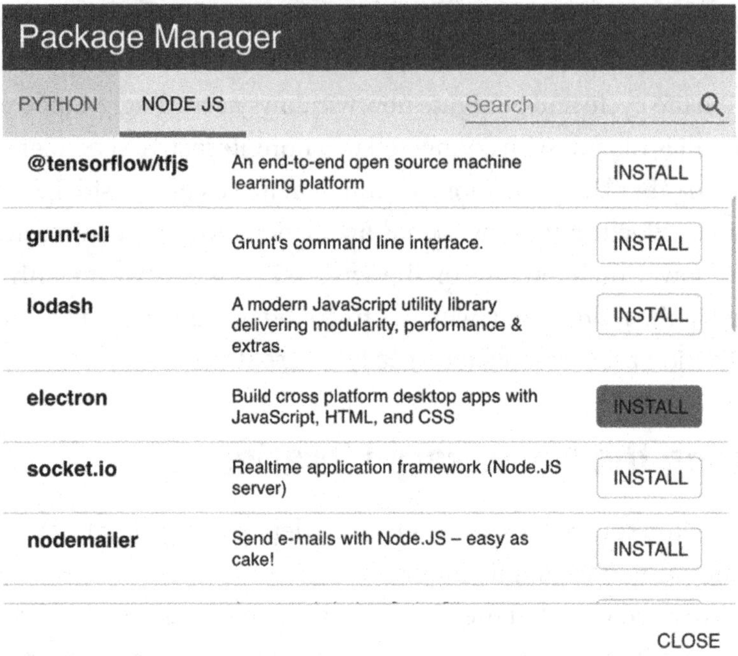

Package Manager			
PYTHON NODE JS		Search	Q
@tensorflow/tfjs	An end-to-end open source machine learning platform	INSTALL	
grunt-cli	Grunt's command line interface.	INSTALL	
lodash	A modern JavaScript utility library delivering modularity, performance & extras.	INSTALL	
electron	Build cross platform desktop apps with JavaScript, HTML, and CSS	INSTALL	
socket.io	Realtime application framework (Node.JS server)	INSTALL	
nodemailer	Send e-mails with Node.JS – easy as cake!	INSTALL	

CLOSE

Figure 3-2. *Installing Electron*

Caution   When this book was written, the latest Electron version does not run on the Raspberry Pi. Therefore, in case you fail to run the application, we recommend you open the SHELL tab and type the command: `sudo npm install -g --unsafe-perm electron@6`. This installs an older version of the library, which is certain to work on the Raspberry Pi device.

Note   If the Raspbian image on the SD card is the Lite version (no UI), we also need to install the necessary libraries to run a user interface.

The main executable that we need to run is *xinit*. This is the application that starts the user interface, which is required to display anything on the screen. You need to understand that any computer or embedded device uses various applications that handle all UI operations. While for your laptop or computer, *xinit* or a similar application is launched at startup, in this case, we have a Lite image that does not do that. Furthermore, when launching the application, we first need to start the user interface.

To install the *xinit* and other related tools, we need to run the following commands in the SHELL tab (Listing 3-6).

Listing 3-6. Install necessary libraries

```
sudo apt-get update
sudo apt-cache search libxss1
sudo apt-get install -y xinit xserver-xorg-core xserver-
xorg-input-all xserver-xorg-video-fbturbo libgtk-3-0 libnss3
libnspr4 libgconf-2-4 libxtst6 libasound2 libxss1 --no-install-
recommends
```

Note   Commands might vary a little depending on the Raspbian version that your Pi runs.

Run the Application

For a simple application, when we click the *Run* button, Wyliodrin STUDIO deploys the project files on the device and executes the **main.js** file. In this specific case, the run process is more complicated. As we already mentioned, we first need to launch the *xinit* process and then execute the source files.

To execute the main file, Wyliodrin STUDIO generates a *makefile* and executes the make run command on the devices. However, if a *makefile* already exists in the project hierarchy, this is used by the platform. We take advantage of this option and create our custom *makefile* to replace the run command (Listing 3-7). The file needs to be placed at the root of the project file hierarchy (Figure 3-3).

Figure 3-3. *The project file hierarchy*

In order for the makefile to be properly run, it is essential to ensure we respect the file format. This requires the file to start with a directive (run in our case), followed by a colon symbol. In the following code, we need to insert one *TAB*, followed by the command to be executed. If we want to execute multiple commands under the same directive, each needs to be placed on a different line, starting with a *TAB*.

Listing 3-7. The makefile

```
run:
        xinit /usr/bin/electron main.js --no-sandbox -- -nocursor
```

Note   A makefile is a configuration file used for build automation. It contains lists of commands grouped under sets of directives.

Inside the *makefile,* we specified the run directive, which starts the application. This command first launches *xinit.*

Further on, we specify the application that we wish the user interface to run, which is Electron (we need to provide the full path to the executable; otherwise xinit will not find it), then we pass the main process file as a parameter to Electron.

The remaining step is to mention that we do not want the cursor to be displayed on the screen and that *xinit* should consider the screen as a touchscreen. This requires us to pass the -nocursor parameter to the *xinit.* Since both *xinit* and Electron can get parameters, we need a way of specifying that the last parameter belongs to *xinit* and not Electron. Therefore, we placed the -- characters before it.

Connect to the Internet

The next step in building the smart signage system is to make it smart and connect it to the Internet. This allows us to download useful information and update the display accordingly.

For this use case, we aim to build a smart weather panel, which would present information such as the weather status or the current temperature. To make sure the data displayed is correct, the panel updates the information every 15 minutes.

As the system we build is similar to the one described earlier, there are no other changes except the ones in the source files. We still use Electron to run the web application, which now becomes a little more complicated.

Application Architecture

The main improvement brought to this application is that we use a web API in order to get real-time data about the weather and then replace the displayed information with the newly obtained one. This requires replacing the static text with one that can be changed from within the application.

Since we have to write JavaScript code to implement the application logic, we can make use of the multitude of frameworks available to ease the development process. You might be familiar with some of these frameworks: jQuery, Angular, Vue. All of these are designed to simplify the manipulation of the HTML files and make it easy to generate dynamic content.

If you are familiar with any of these frameworks, you can implement the one you find the most comfortable to use. In this book, we decided to use Vue. To learn more about this framework and get familiar with it, we recommend going through the Vue.js tutorial.[5]

Source Files

The first file that we need to alter to obtain a smart billboard is **index.html** (Listing 3-8). Here we need to replace the static text with one that changes every time new information is downloaded. This is why we added the *{{weather}}* filed, which is replaced with the value of the *weather* variable during runtime.

Listing 3-8. The interactive HTML source code

```
<!DOCTYPE html>
<html lang="en">
  <head>
    <title>Welcome</title>
    <script src="https://cdn.jsdelivr.net/npm/vue"></script>
    <script src="https://cdnjs.cloudflare.com/ajax/libs/
    axios/0.19.0/axios.js"></script>
  </head>
  <body>
```

---

[5]https://vuejs.org/v2/guide

```
    <div id="app">
        <center> The weather outside is {{weather}}. </center>
        <br>
        <label> {{error}}</label>
    </div>
    <script src="app.js"></script>
  </body>
</html>
```

Additionally, we included two essential libraries in the project: vue, on which the whole application is based, and ajax, which is used to retrieve data from the weather API. Finally, we imported the **app.js** file that we implement next.

Finally, the JavaScript code has to be linked to an element in the HTML file; this is why we created a div having the app ID.

The JavaScript file creates a Vue component that exports the weather variable, which is replaced in the HTML structure. Moreover, due to Vue's properties, each time the variable changes its value, the interface will automatically update (Listing 3-9).

Listing 3-9. Set the application to update according to the weather data

```
var app = new Vue ({
  el: '#app',
  data () {
  return {
    weather: null,
    error: "
  }
},
```

```
created () {
  let getData = async ()=>{
      try{
        let response = await axios.get('https://samples.
        openweathermap.org/data/2.5/weather?q=London,uk&appid=b
        6907d289e10d714a6e88b30761fae22');
        this.weather = response.data.weather[0].main;
      }
      catch (err){
         this.error = err;
      }
    setTimeout (getData, 1000*60*15);
  };
  getData();
}
});
```

Let us break this code into smaller pieces to better understand it.

Listing 3-10. Create a new Vue application

```
var app = new Vue ({
    el: '#app',
    data () {
    return {
     weather: null,
     error: "
    }
  }
```

First, we have to create a new Vue component and assign it to a tag in the HTML file (Listing 3-10). The Vue component receives a JSON object containing various fields. The first field, el, is the link to the tag. We are

using here the jQuery selector[6] names. Next, we have the data field, where
we have to declare all variables that are referenced in the HTML file, in
our case, weather. Finally, we declared a string variable to store any errors
coming from the web API.

Listing 3-11. Get online data

```
created () {
  let getData = async ()=>{
     try{
        let response = await axios.get('https://samples.
        openweathermap.org/data/2.5/weather?q=London,uk&appid=b
        6907d289e10d714a6e88b30761fae22');
        this.weather = response.data.weather[0].main;
     }
     catch (err){
        this.error = err;
     }
   setTimeout (getData, 1000*60*15);
  };
  getData();
}
```

Next, we have the created field, which is a function that is called once
the HTML structure has finished loading (Listing 3-11). Here, we define
the getData() function, which uses the axios module to retrieve data from
the web service. The await keyword stops the function from executing
further commands until the requested information is returned. Next, we
store the data into the weather variable and set the function to run again in
15 minutes, using setTimeout(). In case there are any errors, the catch()

---

[6]www.w3schools.com/jquery/jquery_ref_selectors.asp

function is called, where we store the error in the global variable to be displayed on the screen.

For the weather data, we use one of the open web APIs.[7] In order to use the API, you need to create an account and obtain a token. For testing purposes, we decided to use one of the sample URLs, which works without the need to authenticate yourself. Therefore, we made a GET request to get the data (`response.data`), which looks like in the following structure (Listing 3-12).

Listing 3-12. The response structure

```
{
    "coord":{
        "lon":-0.13,
        "lat":51.51
    },
    "weather":[
        {
            "id":300,
            "main":"Drizzle",
            "description":"light intensity drizzle",
            "icon":"09d"
        }
    ],
    "base":"stations",
    "main":{
        "temp":280.32,
        "pressure":1012,
        "humidity":81,
```

---

[7]https://openweathermap.org

```
    "temp_min":279.15,
    "temp_max":281.15
},
"visibility":10000,
"wind":{
    "speed":4.1,
    "deg":80
},
"clouds":{
    "all":90
},
"dt":1485789600,
"sys":{
    "type":1,
    "id":5091,
    "message":0.0103,
    "country":"GB",
    "sunrise":1485762037,
    "sunset":1485794875
},
"id":2643743,
"name":"London",
"cod":200
}
```

From the obtained data, we extracted the first element from the weather field, then the main field to get Drizzle, which is also the word that appears on the screen once you run the application (Figure 3-4).

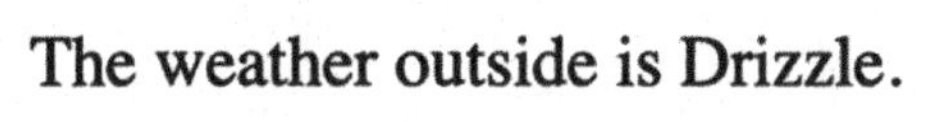

The weather outside is Drizzle.

Figure 3-4. *The resulting interface*

Arrange the Interface

As a final step, to bring our application closer to a billboard system, we improve the user interface by adding a couple of extra elements, such as style definitions, images, and colors.

The first file that we change is **index.html** (Listing 3-13).

Listing 3-13. Improved index.html file

```html
<html lang="en">
<head>
    <title>Welcome</title>
    <style>
    body {background: black; margin: 0; overflow: hidden;
    padding: 0; position:relative; font-size:21px; font-
    weight:300; color:white;}
    #app {margin: auto; overflow: hidden; padding: 0;
    position:relative; width:100%; height:100%;}
      .app-box{top:0; bottom:0; left:0; right:0; margin:auto;
      display:block; padding:30px; position:absolute; height:
      fit-content; width: fit-content;}
      .w-status {padding:50px 0;}
      .error {position:absolute; bottom:0; text-align:center;
      width:100%; padding:20px 0; left:0; right:0;
      background:red; color:white;}
    </style>
    <script src="https://cdn.jsdelivr.net/npm/vue"></script>
    <script src="https://cdnjs.cloudflare.com/ajax/libs/
    axios/0.19.0/axios.js"></script>
</head>
```

```
<body>
    <div id="app">
        <div class="app-box">
            <center>
                <img v-bind:src=imgUrl>
                <div class="w-status">The weather
                outside is {{weather}}.</div>
                <div>The current temperature is
                {{temperature}} Fahrenheit.</div>
            </center>
        </div>
        <label class="error">{{error}}</label>
    </div>
    <script src="app.js"></script>
</body>
</html>
```

Here we first added the <style> tag where we defined various style
elements that are attributed to the tags in the <body> section. Further on,
we added the <img> tag that loads an image. Since we used the v-bind
directive, we can replace the path to the image with a variable that we
change based on the weather. Finally, we added the outside temperature to
the displayed information.

Next, we updated the **app.js** file (Listing 3-14). Here we declared
the temperature variable where we store the temperature returned by
the web service. As the value we get is in kelvin (1K, the standard unit of
measurement for temperature), we applied a formula to obtain Fahrenheit
degrees. We also update the imgUrl variable to store the path to a different
image based on the weather.

Listing 3-14. The complete app.js file

```
var app = new Vue ({
  el: '#app',
  data () {
  return {
    weather: null,
    temperature: 0,
    imgUrl: 'img/sun.png',
    error: 'No errors'
  }
},
created () {
  let getData = async ()=>{
      try{
        let response = await axios.get('https://samples.
        openweathermap.org/data/2.5/weather?q=London,uk&appid=b
        6907d289e10d714a6e88b30761fae22');
        this.weather = response.data.weather[0].main;
        if (this.weather === 'Drizzle' || this.weather === 'Rain')
            this.imgUrl = 'img/rain.png';
        else if (this.weather === 'Sun')
            this.imgUrl = 'img/sun.png';
        this.temperature = response.data.main.temp * 9/5 - 459.67;
      }
      catch (err){
         this.error = err;
      }
    setTimeout (getData, 1000*60*15);
  };
  getData();
}
});
```

The final step to obtaining a working application is to upload the images we use to the project hierarchy. For this, we recommend downloading images that represent different weather types, create a new directory called **img**, inside **UI**, and upload the pictures there.

Tip   In our example we used Flaticon[8] to find nice weather images.

Now, when we run the application, we have a working weather signage system (Figure 3-5).

Figure 3-5.   *The smart signage interface*

---

[8]www.flaticon.com/

Summary

In this chapter, we went through the basics of running a web application interface on the Raspberry Pi to create a smart signage system. This can be used in a multitude of use cases, from the smart weather panel to a traffic monitoring system or an advertisement panel.

Note   The proof-of-concept application developed in this chapter might run into some trouble for very large signage systems or when highly dynamic (video) content needs to be displayed in real time. Computational aspects of the underlying hardware platform need to be taken into account in the design phase of the solution (e.g., transferring, decoding, and displaying MPEG2/MPEG4/WMV video streams in real time on display with a very large number of LEDs or pixels might be very problematic for a Raspberry Pi).

To customize the application, we recommend to read more about the Vue framework and add some CSS to the HTML file. Also, by exploring the *OpenWeather API* or other similar services, you can display all sorts of different data.

CHAPTER 4

Smart Soda Dispenser System

One of the advantages that the IoT brings to many industries is the possibility of remotely monitoring, diagnosing, and controlling various equipment. For industrial systems, this implies that we can prevent or quickly solve malfunctions, while for consumer devices, this also results in more accessible ways of tracking the gadgets and adapting them to the user behavior.

In this chapter, we aim to build a smart soda dispenser, which is connected to the Internet and sends real-time data about the availability of the products to a web service where information is displayed in a graphical interface.

A soda dispenser is just a type of vending machine which provides specific soda products (cans and bottles). While vending machines appeared in England around 1880 with the purpose of selling postcards, they were soon diversified to a varied list of products and after the 1950s became part of the urban landscape in most big cities around the world. The number of soda dispensers specifically exploded with the success of several American soda companies whose business expanded in the United States and Europe, and then worldwide. A similar expansion happened with the advent of bottled water, which needs to be available (and chilled), especially in hot weather. Today, soda dispensers can be found

© Ioana Culic; Alexandru Radovici; Cristian Rusu 2020
I. Culic et al., *Commercial and Industrial Internet of Things Applications with the Raspberry Pi*,
https://doi.org/10.1007/978-1-4842-5296-3_4

in game centers and stadiums, hospitals, schools, and universities, any transportation hubs such as airports and train stations, and, in general, on streets in any dense urban area. Soda fountains had also seen great commercial success from the 1830s when they began to be sold and used in bars and restaurants behind the counter.

Historically, applications similar to soda dispensers are among the first examples of IoT thinking. In 1992, a group of students and researchers from Cambridge University was annoyed with the fact that the coffee pot was in a shared room (the Trojan room) and many times they would walk to this room just to find that the coffee was over. They set up a camera that would photograph the coffee machine three times every minute and would make the photos available to the whole network via a web page. This way, everyone could check the availability of coffee before making their way to the Trojan room. This simple application is referenced today as one of the earliest IoT devices and is viewed as the grandfather of smart dispensing machines.

To build a smart soda dispenser, we extend the notions presented in the previous project, so this time we have an advanced web-based user interface where the user can interact with the touchscreen to choose between different beverages and turn on and off the pump. The amount of drinks consumed is sent to a web service where we can monitor the filling rate of the soda tank. Later, consumption rates collected from multiple dispensers over a long period of time can provide insights into the habits of the customers and the service maintenance times for the machines.

Necessary Components

To build the smart soda dispenser, you will need the following components:

- Raspberry Pi connected to the Internet and to Wyliodrin STUDIO.

- Touchscreen display – Used to show the interface and control the system. We recommend the Raspberry Pi touch display[1]; Pi Hut has a good tutorial on how to connect the display.[2]

- Three KY-019 relays or similar and three DC water pumps[3] – These allow the liquid flow. There is also the option to use only water pumps; it depends on the components you have.

- DC Barrel Adapter.[4]

- 5V power source.

- Breadboard.

- Jumper wires.

Note This is a very simple soda dispenser, meant to detail the IoT software component. For a real machine, the mechanics and control elements are different. Though different, the way the Raspberry Pi interacts with the machine mechanics is more or less similar to this example. It might be either via GPIO (this example), UART, SPI, or I2C. We will discuss these details in the following chapters of this book.

---

[1]www.raspberrypi.org/products/raspberry-pi-touch-display

[2]thepihut.com/blogs/raspberry-pi-tutorials/45295044-raspberry-pi-7-touch-screen-assembly-guide

[3]www.amazon.com/Water-Northbear-Ultra-quiet-Brushless-Submersible/dp/B01N9FNK23

[4]www.sparkfun.com/products/10288

Interactive Soda Dispenser

The first step in building the soda dispenser system is to create the graphical interface that user interacts with. For this, we can start from the example in the previous chapter, where we have built a simple web interface that runs on the Raspberry Pi using the electron framework.

First, we create a new JavaScript application inside Wyliodrin STUDIO. Next, we duplicate the application structure from Chapter 3, where we have a **UI** directory containing a file called **index.html** and another one called **app.js**.

The main.js File

The first file that we have to define is **main.js**. From the previous chapter, we are already familiar with this file, which is a Node.js script that launches the electron application. As the main structure of the application remains the same as the previous one, there is no need to change the contents of the file. However, the system we are building now is more complex, and there is a high chance of errors and debugging required. In case the application we run is still under development, we might need to do some debugging and check console messages and errors that it generates. While for a regular web application this can be done by interacting with the browser with the help of a mouse and keyboard and launching the development console, in our case, there is no way of actually controlling the electron environment in an interactive manner. Therefore, if we want to have the development console launched, we need to specify this from within the main process by adding the following line: `mainWindow.webContents.openDevTools();`

The User Interface

Now that we have configured the electron environment properly, we need to create the user interface. The UI consists of two files: an HTML and a JavaScript file. To obtain an application that is easy to configure and alter, inside the HTML file, we only define design elements such as buttons and labels. Still, we do not populate them with the information. For instance, we specify that we have a round button for each beverage available, but we do not specify the number of buttons or the text to be displayed on each of them. This way, we can think of the HTML as a template that shows the information defined in the JavaScript file. Therefore, if we want to change the number or types of beverages, it is enough to do one change in the app.js file, and this is reflected throughout the application. Similar to the previous application, we use Vue.js, so it is easier to create a dynamic UI. This is why the two files are tightly coupled, and we need to create them simultaneously.

For this application, we display a different button for each beverage type available, a *Pour* button which starts pouring the drink and a *Stop* button.

Display Beverages

In this context, we first create the following **index.html** file, which displays a button for each beverage type (Listing 4-1).

Listing 4-1. The index.html file

```
<!DOCTYPE html>
<html lang="en">
  <head>
    <title>Soda</title>
  </head>
```

```
<body>
  <div id="app">
      <div v-for="beverage of beverages">
          <button v-bind:style="{color: beverage.wcolor,
            background: beverage.bgcolor}">{{beverage.name}}
          </button>
      </div>
      </div>
  <script src="app.js"></script>
  </body>
</html>
```

Now let us take a closer look at the tags used.

First, we created one `<div>` tag that contains all the information displayed and which is linked to the JavaScript application:
`<div id="app">`.

Further on, for each beverage we display, we create a different `<div>` element. To programmatically populate the interface, we included the v-for directive in the `<div>` tag. What this directive does is to iterate in a given array (beverages in our case), and for each element, a different DOM object is created.

The beverages array is defined inside the **app.js** file, which looks like in Listing 4-2.

Listing 4-2. The app.js file

```
const Vue = require ('vue/dist/vue.common.js');
var app = new Vue ({
    el: '#app',
    data: {
      beverages: [
          {name: 'soda', bgcolor: 'darkred', wcolor: 'white'},
          {name:'orange juice', bgcolor: 'orange', wcolor: 'white'},
```

```
        {name: 'water', bgcolor: 'cornflowerblue', wcolor:
        'white'}],
      selection: null
  },
        created() {
  this.selection = this.beverages[0];
 }
});
```

In the **app.js** file, we first import the vue module, and we create a new vue application that is linked to the app element. While in the previous chapter, we imported the vue module using a link referenced in the HTML file, now we install the library on the device and import it using the require() function. This is similar to the installation of the onoff library in the previous chapter.

We then define the beverages array inside the data section. This means the variable that is linked to the vue application can be accessed from the HTML file, also linked to this application.

In the HTML file, we can use the properties of each element to customize the button. To define style elements that are based on variables, we had to use the v-bind directive.

Select Beverage

Once we have the *beverage* buttons defined, we can store the selected drink (Listing 4-3). To achieve this, we have to add a new directive to the buttons: v-on:click="select(beverage)", which calls the select() function each time the button is pressed. As all the buttons call the same function, we add the beverage as a parameter.

Listing 4-3. Click event on the button

```
<button class="juice-type" v-on:click= "select(beverage)"
v-bind:style="{color: beverage.wcolor, background: beverage.
bgcolor}">{{beverage.name}}</button>
```

As usual, the function needs to be declared inside the **app.js** file. Similarly, to the data field, we add a methods field, where we define all functions that can be called from the HTML file, similar to Listing 4-4.

Listing 4-4. The methods defined in the app.js file

```
methods: {
    select (element) {
      this.selection = element;
    }
}
```

Notice that the defined function stores the selected element in a variable. The selection variable needs to be added to the data field (Listing 4-5).

Listing 4-5. The data field

```
data: {
    beverages: [
        {name: 'soda', bgcolor: 'darkred', wcolor: 'white'},
       {name: 'juice', bgcolor: 'orange', wcolor: 'white'},
        {name: 'water', bgcolor: 'cornflowerblue', wcolor:
        'white'}],
      selection: null
  }
```

So far, we can select a beverage, but as selection is null at first, to obtain a proper behavior, we need to assign it a value once the application starts. You might be familiar with this event from the previous chapter, where we started downloading information about the weather once the application was created. In a similar manner, we add the created() function to the vue application, where we assign a value to the selection variable. We had to make sure that selection was previously defined in data, as setting any new property that is not defined in data will not be taken into consideration by vue (Listing 4-6).

Listing 4-6. Initial selection

```
created() {
    this.selection = this.beverages[0];
  }
```

Caution To access variables declared in the data section, you need to use the this.variable format.

Pour Drink

The next step, after selecting the beverage, is to present the Pour and Stop buttons to the user (Listing 4-7).

Listing 4-7. Pour and Stop buttons defined in the index.html file

```
<button v-show="!pouring" v-on:click="pour(true)"> Pour
{{selection.name}} </button>
<button v-show="pouring" v-on:click="pour(false)"> Stop
</button>
```

For both buttons, we call the pour() function, where depending on the parameter, we specify if we should start pouring the beverage or stop the process. However, the trick here is that both buttons should not be visible at once. This is why we included the v-show directive, which depends on the pouring variable. This variable is set to true when *Pour* is pressed and set to false when we press the other button. Similarly, we display a short text when a beverage is pouring: <label v-show="pouring">Pouring {{selection.name}}</label>.

In the JavaScript file, we now define the newly used variable pouring, which is false at first. In the methods section, we declare the pour()function, where pouring changes its value (Listing 4-8).

Listing 4-8. The app.js file

```
const Vue = require ('vue/dist/vue.common.js');
var app = new Vue ({
    el: '#app',
    data: {
      beverages: [
          {name: 'soda', bgcolor: 'darkred', wcolor: 'white'},
          {name:'juice', bgcolor: 'orange', wcolor: 'white'},
          {name: 'water', bgcolor: 'cornflowerblue', wcolor:
          'white'}],
        selection: null,
        pouring: false
    },
    methods: {
        select (element) {
          this.selection = element;
        },
```

```
        pour (action){
            this.pouring = action;
        }
    },
    created() {
        this.selection = this.beverages[0];
    }
});
```

Style the User Interface

The final step in building the user interface is to add some style elements so it looks elegant (Listing 4-9).

Listing 4-9. The final index.html file

```html
<!DOCTYPE html>
<html lang="en">
  <head>
    <title>Welcome</title>
    <style>
      body {background: black; margin: 0; overflow: hidden;
      padding: 0;}
      #app {padding-top: 70px;}
      .select-box {width: 70%; margin: auto; height: 150px;}
      .juice-box {width: 33%; text-align: center; float: left;}
      .juice-type {border: 0; border-radius: 150px; text-align:
      center; width: 140px; line-height: 140px; font-size: 18px;}
      .pour-bt-box {width: 60%; margin: auto; padding-top:
      50px; text-align: center;}
      .pour-bt-box button {text-align: center; color:white;
      border: white 2px solid; padding: 20px 0px; width: 60%;
      background: transparent; font-size: 18px; border-radius: 30px;}
```

```
  .pour-bt-box label {text-align: center; color:yellow;
  padding: 20px 0; margin-top: 30px; width: 60%;
  background: transparent; font-size: 21px; font-weight:
  lighter; display: inline-block;}
    </style>
  </head>
  <body>
    <div id="app">
      <div class="select-box">
        <div class="juice-box" v-for="beverage of beverages">
          <button class="juice-type"
          v-on:click="select(beverage)"
          v-bind:style="{color: beverage.wcolor, background:
          beverage.bgcolor}">{{beverage.name}}</button>
        </div>
      </div>
      <div class="pour-bt-box">
        <button v-show="!pouring" v-on:click="pour(true)">Pour
        {{selection.name}}</button>
        <button v-show="pouring" v-on:click="pour(false)">
        Stop</button>
        <br>
        <label v-show="pouring">Pouring {{selection.name}}</label>
      </div>
    </div>
    <script src="app.js"></script>
  </body>
</html>
```

In the <style> tag we have defined some CSS classes such as app-background, select-box, juice-type, and so on. Each class has specific style characteristics that are applied to the corresponding HTML elements,

resulting in the round and colorful buttons and stylish button borders
(Figure 4-1). The application will be ready to run only after you install the
required modules (next section).

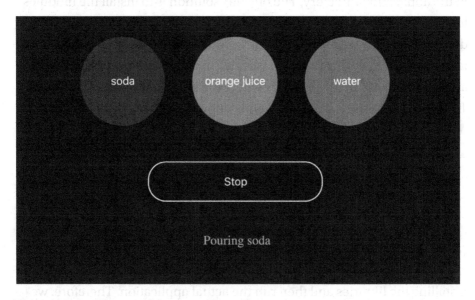

Figure 4-1. *The resulting user interface*

Install Required Modules

The first line in the app.js file uses an external module, vue. Therefore, the
last step required to run the application successfully is to install it. For this,
we need to launch the *Package Manager*, identify the Node.js library in the
dropdown list, and select *install*.

Note   If any of the Node.js libraries you wish to install is not listed
under Package Manager, you can install it by opening the SHELL tab
and entering `sudo npm install -g <package_name>`.

While we installed the necessary module at a global level on the device, the application we run inside electron is not able to access it. Electron works only with modules installed locally, which can be accessed in the application directory. The obvious solution is to install the modules locally. However, this means each time we deploy the application on the device (each time we press *Run*), the modules have to be reinstalled, which takes time. To make the process faster, we make a symbolic link in the application folder to the directory where the global modules are installed. This needs to be done before the application is executed, when the *Run* button is pressed.

Note   In a production environment, the modules are installed at a local level when the application is built. This will be discussed further on in the book.

What we aim to do is to run the necessary configuration commands for installing the libraries and then run the actual application. Therefore, we build our own makefile to specify these two operations (Listing 4-10).

Listing 4-10. The makefile

```
run:
    ln -s /usr/lib/node_modules node_modules
    xinit /usr/bin/electron main.js --no-sandbox --   -nocursor
```

Inside the makefile we specified the run directive which leads to two commands being executed: make a link to the global libraries directory, then launch the application.

Building the Dispenser

The next step in building the smart soda dispenser system is to control the beverage flow. For this, we need to build the physical system that pumps the drinks, which is controlled through the Raspberry Pi.

The Schematic

Usually, soda fountains are built using pump systems, which bring the liquid from the tanks to your cup. In a similar manner, we use smaller water pumps designed for prototyping purposes. The pumps we use are designed to work when connected to a 3–5V power source, which might make you believe that it is enough to connect them to one of the Raspberry Pi's pins. However, the pumps draw a lot of current from the device, and this can lead to malfunctioning of the Pi. Therefore, we connect the pumps to an external power source, and we control them with the help of relays.

Note   A relay is a switch that can be connected to a high-power source and can be controlled using a small current.

The relays we use are connected to both the Raspberry Pi and the 5V power source. For this, we recommend using a power source similar to the Arduino one and connect it using the DC power barrel. The circuit schematic is depicted in Figure 4-2.

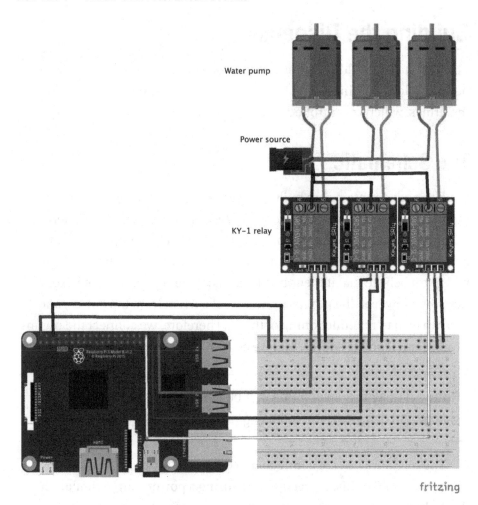

Figure 4-2. *Pump circuit schematic*

Tip   You can connect the same power source to all the three pumps.

The Application

The application that controls the earlier schematic needs to integrate the user interface with the hardware. The relays connected to the Raspberry Pi can be switched on and off by controlling the appropriate digital pins. Therefore, we use the onoff module to control the soda flow.

Note   Usually, web applications are designed to run in the browser and, for security reasons, have no access to the peripherals of the devices that they run on. However, in this case, as we use electron instead of a regular browser, the framework allows us to access and control the Raspberry Pi pins.

Pins Setup

The first step in building the application is to import the onoff library:

```
const Gpio = require('onoff').Gpio;
```

As for each beverage we have a different tank, thus a different pump, we assign the corresponding pin to each element in the beverages array (Listing 4-11).

Listing 4-11. Beverages array with the corresponding pin

```
beverages: [
    {name: 'soda', bgcolor: 'darkred', wcolor: 'white',
    pinNumber: 16},
    {name:'juice', bgcolor: 'orange', wcolor: 'white',
    pinNumber: 20},
    {name: 'water', bgcolor: 'cornflowerblue', wcolor: 'blue',
    pinNumber: 21}]
```

Further on, we can initialize the GPIO pins as output and control them using the writeSync() function. The initialization can be done in the created() function where we iterate the beverage array (Listing 4-12).

Listing 4-12. Pins initialization

```
for (let beverage of this.beverages){
        beverage.pin= new Gpio(beverage.pinNumber, 'out');
}
```

Controlling the Relay

The final step in starting and stopping the beverage pumps is to control the relays connected to the Raspberry Pi. Each time the *Pour* button is pressed, the pump should start running, and when *Stop* is pressed, the pump should stop. Therefore, we insert the pin control line inside the pour() function (Listing 4-13).

Listing 4-13. The pour() function

```
pour (action){
    this.pouring = action;
    if (action)
        this.selection.pin.writeSync (1);
    else
        this.selection.pin.writeSync (0);
  }
```

Once the application is deployed on the device, once you install the necessary modules, you obtain a functioning beverage dispenser.

Note   There might be other ways of controlling the beverage flow that you can try to implement. In either case, the physical system will resume to one or multiple pins that you have to control.

Installing the Modules

As we already mentioned, to control the pins, we imported the onoff module. While the module should already be installed at a global level on the device, it has to be rebuilt to work with the electron environment (electron-rebuild). This requires us to run an extra command before running the application (Listing 4-14).

To be able to run this command, we need to install it: sudo npm install -g --unsafe-perm electron-rebuild.

Finally, when we press the *Run* button, we obtain a working soda dispenser system.

Listing 4-14. The final makefile

```
run:
    ln -s /usr/lib/node_modules node_modules
    electron-rebuild --module-dir=node_modules/onoff
    xinit /usr/bin/electron main.js --no-sandbox --  -nocursor
```

Connecting the System to the Internet

Any IoT system should be, in a way or another, connected to the Internet. In this beverage dispenser case, connecting it to the Internet is essential as we need a way of remotely monitoring these systems.

One of the main components of such a system is the beverage tanks, which need to be refilled regularly at a pace that can ensure that the containers will not get empty during business hours, but also have fresh beverages. To optimize the times at which the tanks should be filled, it is important to monitor the beverage consumption continuously. Also, in the unexpected situation that a tank gets empty, we should be notified instantly to take the appropriate actions.

In this context, we integrate the system with ubidots,[5] a web service specialized in storing data from IoT devices.

Set Up Ubidots Account

Ubidots is a cloud platform designed for storing and displaying data coming from IoT devices. It exposes a REST API that enables its users to interact with the platform from within their applications. In a nutshell, the applications we develop have to make specific requests, leading to data being stored on the ubidots platform. Further on, that information can be displayed in an intuitive manner with the help of graphs and other visual elements.

What we aim to do by using ubidots is to send data about the beverage consumption and display the amount of liquid left in each soda tank. The first step in using the platform is to create an account. The service offers various plans, depending on the usage purpose. For educational purposes, you can get a free account that has limitations, both in the graphs that you can use and in the amount of data that can be stored. For industrial applications, you need to pay to create an account; but you can try a 30-day trial account, which is what we do for this application.

To create a new trial account, we have to select the *Get Started for Free* button (Figure 4-3) and insert some basic details such as the username and email.

---

[5]https://ubidots.com

Figure 4-3. *Create new ubidots account*

Once the account is created, a token is generated. This is the authentication element that needs to be attached to all request messages. To obtain the token, when logged in, click the profile settings and select *API Credentials* (Figure 4-4). The token field will show up, and we can copy it.

Figure 4-4. *Get account token*

Initialize Widget Values

As we obtained all the necessary information, we can move on to building the request messages to push data to the ubidots platform. To do this, we need to understand how the information is structured on the platform. Ubidots uses the following main elements:

- Devices – The edge devices that send data to the platform

- Widgets – Graphical elements that display data

- Dashboards – A collection of widgets

- Variables – Identifiers for data streams sent to the platform

First, we define the message header, where we have to add the token and the URL for the request. The last part of the URL (raspberry in our case) is the name of the device that we plan to send data from, and is registered in the ubidots platform under this name (Listing 4-15).

Listing 4-15. Ubidots configuration

```
const ubidotsHeader = {'X-Auth-Token': 'your_token'};
const ubidotsURL = 'https://industrial.api.ubidots.com/api/
v1.6/devices/raspberrypi';
```

The next step is to send the initial information about the total liquid amount stored in the tanks. The tanks that we plan to use for prototyping purposes have two-liter capacity, so we initialize each one to 2000 milliliters. As we have three different tanks, which results in three different data sources, we add three variables to the application. We make the initial requests in the `created()` function.

The request that adds a new variable value to the application has the following characteristics:

- URL – `https://industrial.api.ubidots.com/api/`
  `v1.6/devices/{{source_device}}`

- Type – POST

- Payload – {variable1_name:variable1_value, variable2_
  name: variable2_value}

- Header: Header containing authentication token

The first step is to generate the payload message, which has to contain three fields for all three data sources. Further on, we will have to build the request message and make the actual request to the platform (Listing 4-16).

Listing 4-16. The request to ubidots

```
let payload = {};
    for (let beverage of this.beverages){
        beverage.pin= new Gpio(beverage.pinNumber, 'out');
        payload[beverage.id] = 2000;
    }
try{
let result = await axios.post (ubidotsURL, payload,
{headers:ubidotsHeader});
console.log (result);
}
catch (err){
    console.error (err);
}
```

Compute the Liquid Amount

Now that the initial values are set up, we have to compute the amount of
liquid that is consumed from each tank and send that data to the ubidots
platform (Listing 4-17).

Listing 4-17. The final app.js file

```
const Gpio = require('onoff').Gpio;
const Vue = require ('vue/dist/vue.common.js');
const axios = require ('axios');
const child_process = require ('child_process');
const fs = require ('fs');

let startDate;
const ubidotsHeader = {'X-Auth-Token': your_token', "Content-
Type": "application/json"};
```

```
const ubidotsURL = 'https://industrial.api.ubidots.com/api/
v1.6/devices/raspberrypi';

var app = new Vue ({
    el: '#app',
    data () {
    return {
      beverages: [
          {name: 'soda', bgcolor: 'darkred', wcolor: 'white',
          pinNumber: 16},
          {name:'juice', bgcolor: 'orange', wcolor: 'white',
          pinNumber: 20},
          {name: 'water', bgcolor: 'cornflowerblue', wcolor:
          'white', pinNumber: 21}],
        selection: null,
        pouring: false
    }
  },
  methods:{

    select(element) {
      this.selection = element;
    },
    async pour(action){
      if (action){
          this.pouring = true;
          this.selection.pin.writeSync (1);
          startDate = Date.now();
      }
      else{
          this.pouring = false;
          this.selection.pin.writeSync (0);
```

```
            let seconds = (Date.now() - startDate)/1000;
            let mililiters = seconds * 10
            let ubidotsVariable = {};
            ubidotsVariable[this.selection.name] = - mililiters;
            try{
                let result = await axios.post (ubidotsURL,
                ubidotsVariable, {headers:ubidotsHeader});
                console.log (result);
            }
            catch (err){
                console.error (err);
            }
        }
    }},
    async created() {

            this.selection = this.beverages[0];
            let payload = {};
            for (let beverage of this.beverages){
                beverage.pin= new Gpio(beverage.pinNumber, 'out');
                payload[beverage.name] = 2000;
                try{
                    let result = await axios.post (ubidotsURL,
                    payload, {headers:ubidotsHeader});
                    console.log (result);
                }
                catch (err){
                    console.error (err);
                }
            }
        }
});
```

To compute how much beverage is disposed, we have to compute the period during which the pump is functioning and multiply it by how much soda runs during that time. For this, we declared startDate, a global variable that is updated each time the *Start* button is pressed. Also, we send the negative value as this needs to be subtracted from the total capacity.

The final step is to send the computed amount to the ubidots platform, which is done when the *Stop* button is pressed.

Caution   Make sure the axios module is installed using the Package Manager.

Create the Dashboard

When the first request is made to the ubidots platform, the device and the variables used in the request are automatically registered. This is why we first have to start the application and then create the dashboard where we plan to see the data.

To create a new dashboard, we select *Data* ➤ *Dashboards* and hit the *Add a new Dashboard* button. Once the dashboard is created, we add three widgets displaying the soda tanks (*Add new widget* ➤ *Tank*). For each tank, we add the corresponding variable (Figure 4-5).

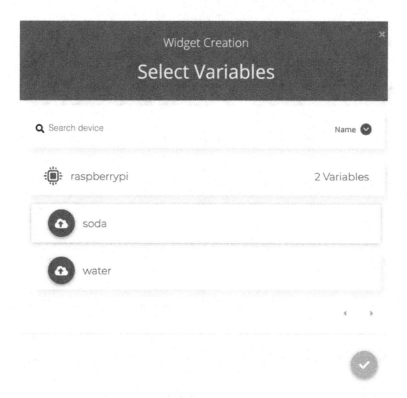

Figure 4-5. *Add variable to widget*

The next step is to set the other widget parameters (Figure 4-6) such as name, range value (from 0 to 2000), and aggregation method (choose *Sum* instead of *Last Value*).

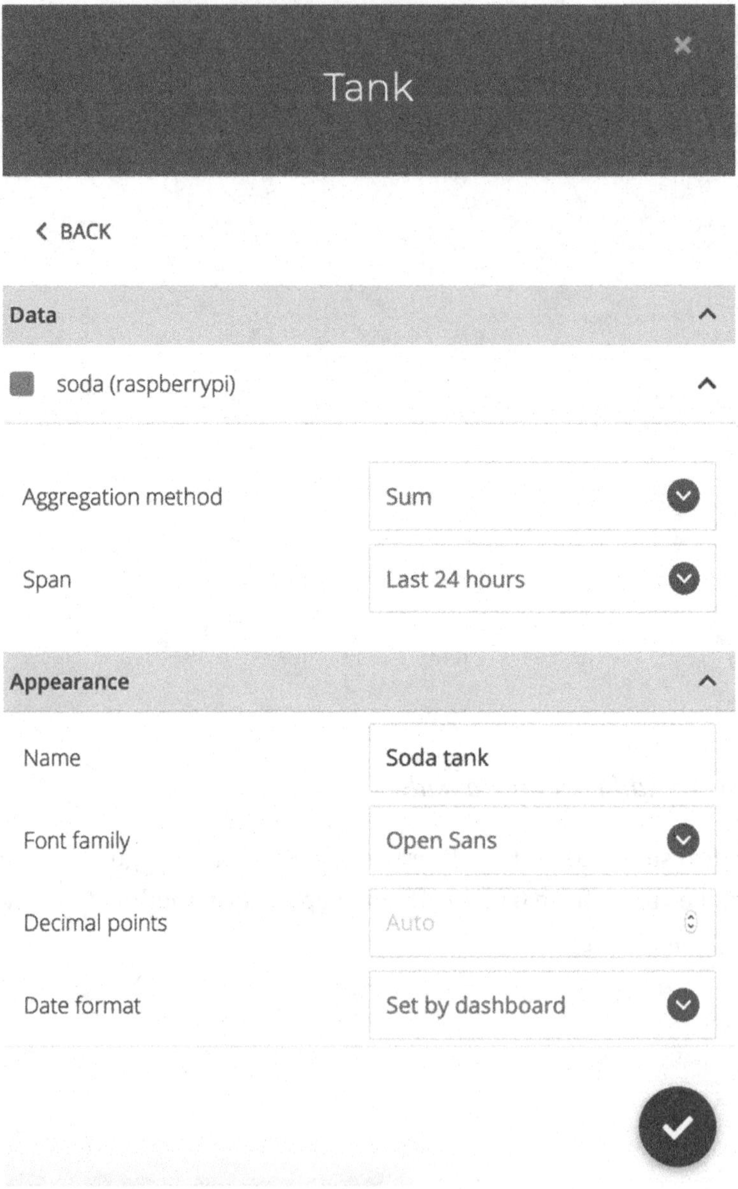

Figure 4-6. *Tank widget properties*

Now, as we turn the pump on and off, the ubidots platform displays the amount of liquid left in the tank (Figure 4-7).

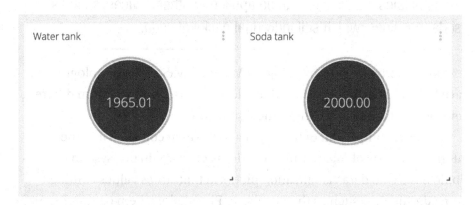

Figure 4-7. *Live dashboard*

Tip   Each time you reset the application, the `created()` function is called, which will add 2000 milliliters to each tank. We recommend you set the widget time span based on when the application is launched. For a real device, it would be a good idea to store the values between software restarts.

Summary

In this chapter, we used simple hardware and software elements to prototype a soda dispenser machine. While such systems seem complicated and difficult to build, by connecting the Raspberry Pi's digital pins to three water pumps, we managed to control the liquid flow from our application.

Note   While the project in this chapter builds a soda fountain, the IoT principles we discuss can be applied to other devices, such as soda machines, which sell individual packs of soda.

On the software side, by using HTML and JavaScript technologies, we have built an intuitive interface that allows the user to select from different beverages available and control the liquid flow.

The final component of the application, which connects it to the Internet, consists of integrating the ubidots platform in our system. Ubidots is a web data visualization platform that stores values coming from edge devices such as the Raspberry Pi and plots them on graphs. As the platform can be accessed using a browser, it enables us to monitor the soda dispenser's status at any time and help us prevent malfunctions and undesired events.

CHAPTER 5

Smart Advertising System

Another area where IoT technologies can make a huge impact is the advertising industry. By taking advantage of the integrated tracking solutions available in this field, commercials and advertisements can be more particular and adapted to the public or even to individuals. We can already think of devices that enable such advancements: smartwatches that can suggest fitness products tailored to your habits, or gas stations that display commercials while you fuel your car. Many search engines and social media services collect and sell search and personal data of users to advertisers who are then able to provide a custom advertising experience. Another concrete example is the Amazon Echo device that monitors users' preferences and can play personalized commercials.

The modern advertising industry is powered by targeted advertising (including microtargeting) and personalized marketing techniques. Because of the increase in the number of mobile devices, traditional forms of advertising (like newspapers) are quickly replaced by online advertising, which is far more effective.

Most modern advertising techniques are based on two general steps: collect historical data and then analyze the data to provide the best future advertising options. In terms of data collecting, the most successful approach is web tracking, including saving geolocation information,

© Ioana Culic; Alexandru Radovici; Cristian Rusu 2020
I. Culic et al., *Commercial and Industrial Internet of Things Applications with the Raspberry Pi*,
https://doi.org/10.1007/978-1-4842-5296-3_5

browser cookies, canvas fingerprinting, mouse tracking, user input logging (from the keyboard or touchscreen), and so on. In fact, even historically, web traffic was among the first information that logged user's movement online since the advent of the World Wide Web (WWW) in the early 1990s. Once the data is collected, it is analyzed using modern machine learning and big data techniques to find past trends and to predict future behavior. The purpose is double: identify personalized advertising for each user who is tracked in real time and identify global trends to explain the behavior of particular groups of people.

With the advent of IoT technologies, marketers have new tools to understand and influence consumers. Sensors can track people in stores and understand their shopping patterns, advanced facial recognition can analyze the satisfaction levels of consumers, real-time personalized advertising can target individuals to maximize the probability of them making a purchase, and recommendation systems that aggregate huge amounts of data can provide accurate predictions of future shopping needs which consumers might currently not even be aware of.

Note   When building such systems, it is crucial to keep in mind aspects related to user privacy and GDPR compliance. Such devices should always inform users about the data they collect and give them the possibility to opt out of having their preferences monitored.

In this chapter, we leverage IoT technologies to build a simple advertising system that adapts the content based on the person in front of the display. The system monitors the surroundings and uses a third-party service to extract data about the people around. Based on the obtained information, it displays a specific picture or set of pictures.

Necessary Components

In order to build the smart advertising system, you will need the following components:

- Raspberry Pi connected to the Internet and to Wyliodrin STUDIO.

- Any display that can be connected via HDMI.

- Raspberry Pi camera module (Figure 5-1).

- USB camera module.

- PIR motion sensor.

Note   We use both the Raspberry Pi and a USB camera module to take pictures, so it is enough to have one of the two to be able to build this project.

Most of the APIs you integrate into your project, including the ones we use in this book, are under continuous development. As such, the way to use and call these APIs changes over time. We highly recommend that before you start the project development you check the latest API documentation. Concerning this chapter, we are aware that while writing this text the Microsoft's Azure Cognitive Services API is undergoing significant changes (switching to v2.0) and therefore the steps we describe in this chapter might differ from the latest release. Please check the latest official documentation of the API.

Figure 5-1. *Pi Camera module[1]*

Gathering Surrounding Information

The system that we are building relies on gathering information about who is watching the commercials it displays. Therefore, the first step in building it is to implement the data collection mechanism, which, in this case, implies taking pictures at regular intervals using the Pi Camera.

---

[1]www.amazon.com/Raspberry-Pi-Camera-Module-Megapixel/dp/B01ER2SKFS

Connect the Camera Module

The Raspberry Pi camera module, released by the Raspberry Pi Foundation, is specially designed to be connected to the Pi so we can easily use the board to take pictures or film videos. The current version of the camera consists of a Sony IMX219 8-megapixel sensor and can take high-definition pictures. It is widely used in various IoT applications, such as home surveillance systems.

Note   For systems requiring taking pictures during the night, we recommend using the Pi NoIR Camera, which lacks in image quality but can be used in the dark.

Connecting any of the cameras to the Raspberry Pi is an easy process as the board has a slot dedicated to this (Figure 5-2).

Figure 5-2. *Camera module slot*

To connect the camera to the Pi, we simply need to lift the plastic clip, insert the cable, and push back down the clip. For the camera to work, the circuits exposed on the ribbon cable need to be in direct contact with the opposite side of the plastic clip. Figure 5-3 depicts the correct orientation when connecting the camera to the Pi.

Caution   Make sure you connect the camera when the Raspberry Pi is not connected to a power supply. Otherwise, there is a slight risk of producing a short circuit that can fry the camera or the Pi.

Figure 5-3. Camera module connected to the Raspberry Pi

Enable the Camera

By default, the Raspberry Pi is not set to detect the camera once this is connected. Therefore, we have to enable the camera option, which activates the driver that allows us to control the module.

To do this, we need to open a SHELL tab inside Wyliodrin STUDIO and type the command sudo raspi-config (Figure 5-4). From the menu that shows up, we have to select the fifth option, *Interfacing Options*, then select *P1 Camera*. This shows a dialog asking if we want the camera interface to be enabled or not. We select *Yes* and exit the menu. For the changes to take place, we also need to reboot the device.

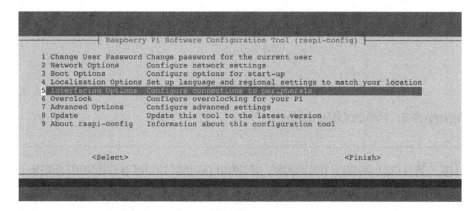

Figure 5-4. *Configure the Pi Camera*

The Code

Once the camera is connected, and the driver is enabled, we can move forward to writing the code that takes pictures.

The architecture of the application we build in this chapter is similar to the ones we designed previously. It is a web application that runs on top of the electron framework. Therefore, we create the folder hierarchy presented in Figure 5-5. First, we need to create the **main.js** file, which is designed to launch the application. Further on, we will create the directory where the source code for the interface resides. As usual, we call that folder UI and add the **index.html** and **main.js** files there. Finally, we need to create the **makefile** so at runtime the **node_modules** folder is linked to the project, the onoff library is rebuilt for electron, and the application is run using xinit.

Figure 5-5. *Project hierarchy*

Tip   You can clone a previously created project under a different name so you can keep the structure and the **makefile** and **main.js** files.

The index.html File

For this use case, the HTML file is relatively simple as we just display an image on the screen (Listing 5-1). For now, for testing purposes, we display the picture that the camera takes. This is the easiest way to check that the code runs accordingly and picture files are saved.

In the HTML file, we use the <img> tag that receives the image file to be displayed in *base64* format and adapts it to the width and height according to the display we use. We decided to load the image file contents in a variable and then pass it to be displayed on the screen, so the image is loaded instantly by the interface. In the classic case, when a link to the image file is specified in the <img> tag, for a large image, the browser might take some time to completely load it on the screen, risking displaying the image partially for a short time.

Once the Electron framework loads the HTML file, we need to specify when the image file has changed to reload the resource. This is why we used the v-bind directive, which allows us to pass the image variable instead of the actual image.

When a new picture is taken, we change the value of image and the Vue framework ensures the new image is loaded onto the screen.

Listing 5-1. The index.html file

```
<!DOCTYPE html>
<html lang="en">
  <head>
    <title>Welcome</title>
  </head>
  <body>
    <div id="app">
    <img v-bind:src= "'data:image/jpeg;base64,'+image"
    height="450" width="760"/>
    </div>
    <script src="app.js"></script>
  </body>
</html>
```

The app.js File

Once the camera module was enabled on the Raspberry Pi, we can choose from several libraries and executables to control it. One of the most used utilities is the raspistill CLI tool.

The basic usage command to take a picture using raspistill is raspistill -o <file_name>.

Since the application we develop is built using Node.js, and it is difficult to find up-to-date modules for controlling the Pi Camera, we run the `raspistill` executable from within our application to take pictures. For this, we first need to import the `child_process` module.

`child_process` is a Node.js module that enables the creation of new processes. This way, we can run executables from our application. In this case, the executable that we wish to run is `raspistill`.

There are several functions available for executing a child process. In our case, we can use the `exec()` function, which receives the full command to be executed as a parameter.

After the picture was taken (the child process completes), we read the new image file and store the result in the `image` variable. We use the base64 encoding to store the data. To achieve this, we imported the `fs-extra` module: `const fs = require ('fs-extra');`

Note   Base64 is one of the most popular encodings for sending binary data over text channels.

`fs-extra` is an external Node.js module that enables the interaction with the file system. Using this module, developers can create or delete files and directories and manipulate them. While the Node.js framework includes the `fs` module, we decided to use `fs-extra` because of the asynchronous functions. As such, we use the `await` syntax instead of callbacks, making the code easier to follow.

To install the `fs-extra` module, we need to open a new SHELL tab and type the command: `sudo npm install -g fs-extra`.

Since there is the risk of failure while taking the picture or reading the resulted file, we use the `try-catch` block, so the application does not crash if an error appears.

Note   Both exec() and readFile() are non-blocking functions.
We use the await keyword to ensure the following command is
executed only after the function returns.

For now, there is no external trigger for when the pictures should
be taken; we just aim to obtain a system that periodically checks the
environment. In this case, we start taking pictures once the application is
created. Therefore, we insert the new lines of code in the created() function.
We use the setInterval() function to take a picture every 15 seconds
(Listing 5-2).

Note   You can change the time interval between two pictures being
taken, but we suggest you leave at least five seconds between
two consecutive pictures. Otherwise you might increase the
computational burden placed on the camera.

Listing 5-2. The app.js file

```
const Vue = require ('vue/dist/vue.common.js');
const child_process = require ('child_process');
const fs = require ('fs-extra');

let index = 0;
var app = new Vue ({
    el: '#app',
    data(){
        return {
                image:"
        };
    },
```

```
created() {
  let takePicture = async ()=>{
      try{
          let command = 'raspistill -n -o /home/pi/image';
          await child_process.exec (command);
          this.image = await fs.readFile('/home/pi/image', {
          encoding: 'base64' });

      }
      catch(err){
          console.error (err);
      }
    setTimeout(takePicture, 15000);
  };
  takePicture ();
}
});
```

We declared the imgPath variable to the data field so we can reference it in the HTML file. Every time the variable changes, vue ensures the new value is replaced in the HTML file, and the corresponding element is reloaded. However, this can only work if we store each picture under a different name, implying a change in the variable's value. This is why we also created a global variable that increments its value for each picture.

Note   Before taking a picture, the camera does a five seconds preview, which shows up on the screen. In order to deactivate this, add the -n parameter to the command: `raspistill -n -o path`.

What is left is to run the application and notice the camera taking a picture every 15 seconds, which is displayed on the screen.

Note   The previous block of code is not efficient as each time a new picture is taken, a new file is stored on the device. We used this code for testing purposes, but if you plan to use it in a production environment, make sure you delete all files that are no longer used.

Personalize the Content

At this point, we have an application that takes pictures every 15 seconds using the Raspberry Pi camera module. To obtain the smart advertisement system we desire, we have to analyze each picture and extract information such as the age and gender of the people in front of the display.

Set Up Microsoft Cognitive Services Account

Similarly to the previous chapters, we use a web service to analyze the pictures. One of the most popular such services is *Microsoft's Azure Cognitive Services*. These services rely on machine learning algorithms developed by Microsoft to solve AI problems related to natural language processing, decision-making, speech analysis, search engines, and image and video processing.

Out of the five available service categories from the cognitive services API, we are interested in the one related to vision. This API enables us to extract information from pictures so we can identify the characteristics of the people we are addressing.

To use cognitive services, a paid account is required. However, for seven days, Microsoft gives you the possibility of using a trial account, which allows you to test the API without any charge.

To create a new account, we need to access the following link: `https://azure.microsoft.com/en-us/services/cognitive-services/face/` and hit the *Try Face* button (Figure 5-6). This opens a three-step menu.

Figure 5-6. *The Cognitive Services platform*

First, we need to select the login type. For now, we aim to test the API, so we select the Guest option, which allows us to use the API for seven days for free (Figure 5-7). The next step requires you to sign in using a Microsoft or other third-party account.

Try Cognitive Services for free

Guest	Free Azure account	Existing Azure account
7-day trial	**$0/month**	**Already have an Azure account?**
Evaluate Cognitive Services for free	Try with an Azure free account	
Get started	Sign up	Sign in
• No credit card required • No data saved after trial	• Get $200 in credits on Azure • Free access that never expires • Data and customizations saved	• Full SLA report • Enterprise grade performance • Full Azure product integration • Scale up seamlessly as needed

Figure 5-7. *Select account type*

Once the sign-in process is completed, you are directed to a page displaying two authentication keys. Also, the service sends you an email containing more information about the API documentation and a link to retrieving your authentication details (Figure 5-8).

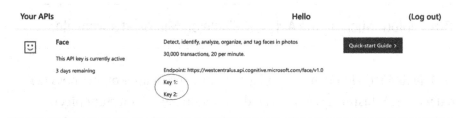

Figure 5-8. *Retrieve account keys*

The two authentication keys are essential for building the application as they are the ones granting us access to the vision API. Similarly to the web services we used before, *Microsoft Cognitive Services* requires us to add one of the two keys to the header of the request sent to the service. This way, the server can identify the account associated with the request and ensure that we have permission to use the service.

Besides the authentication information, we can also visualize the endpoint that we should access in order to use the API. Depending on the account details, a different endpoint can be assigned. This is why it is important to make sure you use the one associated with your account.

Note   In this chapter we use an older version of the API (v1.0 instead of v2.0). The newer version, which has been released recently, works in the same manner; it just requires a different account requesting for more authentication details.

Process the Picture

Now that we have created a trial account for accessing the vision API, we can integrate this into our application so the pictures we take are processed.

Tip   Information on the API is available on Microsoft's web site.[2]

The first step in using the API is to define the header of the message that we send (Listing 5-3). The header contains two important pieces of information: the authentication key and the type of the payload being transmitted. Up until now, we have sent only raw data structured under JSON format to the servers. This is because the information being transmitted has consisted of numbers and text. In this case, we have to send the whole picture to the web service. Therefore, the type of packet being transmitted is `octet-stream`.

Listing 5-3. Azure package header

```
const azureHeader = {'Content-Type': 'application/octet-stream',
  'Ocp-Apim-Subscription-Key': '<your_key>'};
```

Next, we define the URL that we have to access in order to request the image to be processed. This URL consists of the endpoint associated with your account, followed by the path to the specific request, then followed by specific parameters.

In our case, the path is `endpoint + /detect` since we aim to recognize facial characteristics from the picture. For this request, the parameters define the features that we wish to extract from the image. We can choose various parameters, such as `faceAttributes` or `recognitionModel`.

---

[2]`https://docs.microsoft.com/en-us/azure/cognitive-services/face/`
`APIReference`

For our use case, we are interested in extracting `faceAttributes`, more specifically, the gender of the people in the picture. In the case of a more complex application, we can specify multiple attributes from age, gender, wearing glasses, emotion analysis, and so on.

In our application we add the line `const azureURL = 'https://westcentralus.api.cognitive.microsoft.com/face/v1.0/detect?returnFaceAttributes=gender';`

Caution   Remember to replace the endpoint with the one generated for your account.

In the preceding example, each picture was stored as a different file so it can be easily displayed in the browser. However, in this case, the images are taken only to be processed by the cognitive services API. Once a picture is processed, it can be replaced with another one having the same name. Therefore, we use the `raspistill` command with a static parameter as the file path. The result is that each new picture replaces the previous one, saving space and ensuring we do not store more pictures than necessary. The image file is stored in the **/home/pi** directory under the name **img.jpg**.

Once the image file is generated, we have to store it in a buffer so we can send it to the web service (Listing 5-4).

Listing 5-4. The takePicture() function

```
created() {
    let takePicture = async ()=>{
        try{
            let command = 'raspistill -o /home/pi/image';
            await child_process.exec (command);
            let imageBuffer = await fs.readFile ('/home/pi/
            image');
```

```
            let result = await axios.post (azureURL,
            imageBuffer, {headers:azureHeader});
            if (result.data.length > 0){
                console.log(result.data[0].faceAttributes.gender);
            }
            setTimeout(takePicture, 15000);
        }
        catch(err){
            console.log (err.response);
        }
    };
    takePicture ();
}
```

Finally, once we have the file contents, we can make the request to the Microsoft service. For this, we use the axios module (`const axios = require ('axios')`), as in the previous chapters. We make a POST request and send the file contents as payload.

The result consists of an array of detected faces. Each face has an `id` associated with it and the requested attributes. To keep the application simple, we pick only the first identified face and extract the gender from the obtained structure.

Personalize the Content

The final step in building the smart advertising system is to display content according to the results from the cognitive services API.

To achieve this, we created a folder called img inside UI. Here we placed two pictures, one targeting females and another one targeting males. Based on what we have created so far, we now wish to read one of the two pictures and display its contents on the screen.

While the **index.html** file remains the same, inside **app.js** (Listing 5-5), we check what the response from the cognitive services is, and based on that, we read one file or another. We also increased the time between taking and saving two pictures as we do not want to have images changing too quickly.

Listing 5-5. The app.js file

```javascript
const Vue = require ('vue/dist/vue.common.js');
const child_process = require ('child_process');
const fs = require ('fs-extra');
const axios = require ('axios');
const path = require ('path');

const azureHeader = {'Content-Type': 'application/octet-stream',
 'Ocp-Apim-Subscription-Key': '<your_key>'};
const azureURL = 'https://westcentralus.api.cognitive.
microsoft.com/face/v1.0/detect?returnFaceAttributes=gender';

var app = new Vue ({
    el: '#app',
    data(){
        return {
               image:"
        };
    },
  async created() {
    try{
        this.image = await fs.readFile (path.join(__dirname,
        'img', 'male.png'), {encoding:'base64'});
    }
```

```
    catch (err){
        console.log (err);
    }
    let takePicture = async ()=>{
        try{
            let command = 'raspistill -o /home/pi/image';
            await child_process.exec (command);
            let imageBuffer = await fs.readFile ('/home/pi/
            image');
            let result = await axios.post (azureURL,
            imageBuffer, {headers:azureHeader});
            if (result.data.length > 0){
                if (result.data[0].faceAttributes.gender ===
                'female')
                    this.image = await fs.readFile (path.
                    join(__dirname, 'img', 'female.png'),
                    {encoding:'base64'});
                else
                    this.image = await fs.readFile (path.
                    join(__dirname, 'img', 'male.png'),
                    {encoding:'base64'});
            }
            setTimeout(takePicture, 30000);
        }
        catch(err){
            console.log (err.response);
        }
    };
    takePicture ();
  }
});
```

Now you can run the application and try out the smart advertising system you have just built.

Note   Remember to create the makefile associated to the project.

Tip   For more accuracy, you can take into account all recognized faces and count the dominant gender. You can also consider more attributes such as age or emotion analysis.

Remotely Update Source Pictures

So far, we have created a system that can display different pictures depending on the people in front of the display. To obtain a fully autonomous, smart advertising system, we need to ensure that commercials can be updated without directly interacting with the devices. Therefore, we need to integrate a web service into our application so pictures are stored remotely and can be quickly updated. In this case, all working devices download the images from the cloud, and each time a picture is changed, this automatically reflects in the system.

To achieve this, we use Google Drive to store the pictures. We selected Google Drive as it is widely used and does not require a new Google account to be created in order to integrate it into our apps. However, we need to do some extra setup so we can authenticate ourselves and integrate the REST API into the application.

Create a Google Service Account

To authenticate applications with Google Drive, the system uses OAuth 2.0. While for UI applications, this implies a login screen that generates the authentication credentials once the user logs in successfully, in our case, we need to authenticate the server application to Google Drive. For this, we need to create a *service account.*

To get started, we first need to access the developer console page.[3] Here, we need to create a new service account. To do this, we create a new project (Figure 5-9).

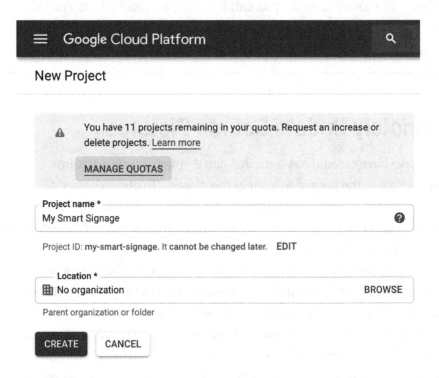

Figure 5-9. *Create a new project*

Once it is created, we are redirected to the project dashboard, where we can create a new service account by clicking the blue button on top of the screen (Figure 5-10). This launches a new form requesting for account details, such as name and description. The service account ID is automatically generated based on the data we insert.

---

[3]https://console.developers.google.com/iam-admin/serviceaccounts

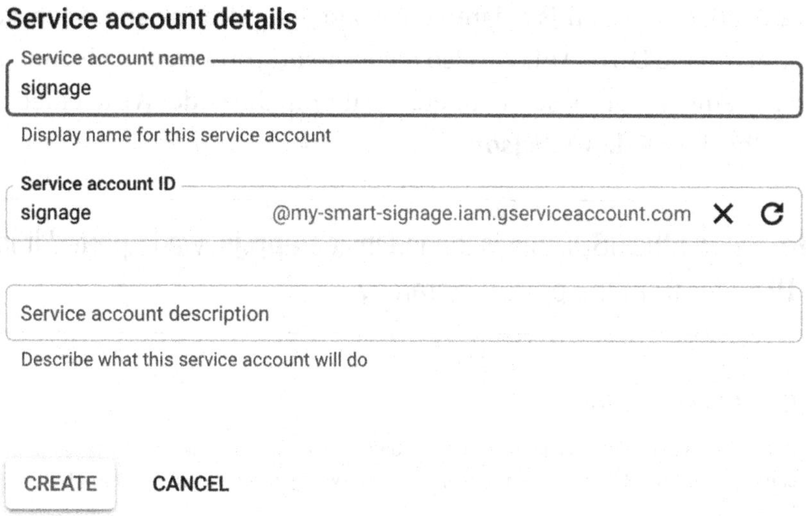

Service account details

Service account name
signage

Display name for this service account

Service account ID
signage   @my-smart-signage.iam.gserviceaccount.com   ✕ ↻

Service account description

Describe what this service account will do

CREATE   CANCEL

Figure 5-10. *Create new service account*

The next step in creating the service account is to specify the permissions. Here, we select project ➤ owner as role. The final step is to create the authentication key. This generates a pair of private-public keys that we can use to authenticate. After we click the *create key* button, a menu appears asking for the type of file to be downloaded (Figure 5-11). We select *JSON* and hit *Create*. This starts the download of a JSON file that contains information about the service account we have just created. Besides the private key, the file also contains the project ID, the client ID, and email, and other details required for authenticating the application with the Google service.

We need to import this file into the Node.js application so we can start using the Google Drive API. We also recommend you save the file under a different name, so it is easier to reference it from the code. We decided to rename the file **credentials.json**.

Note   Since the JSON file is loaded inside **app.js**, we imported it in the **UI** folder from the project hierarchy.

Create key (optional)

Download a file that contains the private key. Store the file securely because this key can't be recovered if lost. However, if you are unsure why you need a key, skip this step for now.

+ CREATE KEY

DONE   CANCEL

Figure 5-11. *Create a new key*

Upload Files on Google Drive

To make the content easy to change, we create three files on Google Drive:

- Two image files – The image files that are displayed in the interface; we delete the files from the application source and upload them on Google Drive.

- A Google spreadsheet – Here we store the categories based on which we display different images and the link to the image associated.

First, we need to upload the image files and ensure they can be accessed by the application. For this, we need to launch the sharing options and add the service account email that was generated previously (Figure 5-12).

Tip   You can find the service account email in the **credentials.JSON** file.

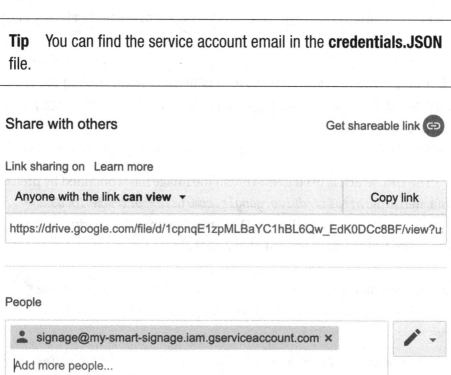

Figure 5-12. *Share image file*

Next, we create the Google spreadsheet file, which has two columns: category and URL (Table 5-1). In the table, we insert male and female as category, while for the URL we need to generate the sharing address that allows the file to be downloaded.

Table 5-1. *The Google Drive spreadsheet*

category	url
male	https://drive.google.com/uc?export=download&id=...
female	https://drive.google.com/uc?export=download&id=...

Caution   The URL that Google Drive generates when sharing the file can be used to open a web page that displays it, but not to directly download the file.

The URL which is used to download the image file is obtained by prefix concatenating: *https://drive.google.com/uc?export=download&id=* with the file ID. To obtain the file ID, we need to open the sharing options again. The ID is in the share link (Figure 5-13).

Figure 5-13. *Get the file ID*

Integrate Google Drive API in the Application

To integrate Google Drive into the application, we first need to read the spreadsheet to get the categories and the associated URLs. Further on, we have to download the pictures and display them on the screen. To be more efficient and reduce the API calls, we can download all the pictures at a specific time interval.

Tip   In real-world situations, updates are usually made during the night, or at a moment when the system is not in heavy use. In our case, for testing purposes, we re-download the pictures every minute.

The interaction with the Google Drive API can be done via simple REST calls. However, the authentication process is complex and requires multiple operations to be done. In this context, we decided to import the google-spreadsheet module, which takes care of the authentication process and also enables reading the spreadsheet's contents using a simple function.

The first step in using the module is to install it. For this, we open a new SHELL tab and type the following command: `sudo npm install -g google-spreadsheet`.

Next, we import the module in our application: `const GoogleSpreadsheet = require('google-spreadsheet');`

To authenticate with the Google Drive API, we need to store the contents of the credentials.json file. Since the file contains a JSON structure, we can import it like any other library: `const credentials = require ('./credentials.json');`

To read the spreadsheet, we need to create a `GoogleSpreadsheet` object. For this, we have to pass the file's ID. Similarly to the image files, the ID can be obtained from the sharing preferences window: `var doc = new GoogleSpreadsheet ('<file id>');`

The next step is to authenticate with the Google service and read the spreadsheet's contents. This is done in the `created()` function. By using `useServiceAccountAuth()`, we can pass the credentials object as a parameter and let the library handle all the authentication. Further on, we call the getRows() function, which receives a callback as the second parameter. There we can manipulate the rows.

For each spreadsheet row, using axios, we make a request that downloads the image. The image is stored in base64 encoding in the pictures structure so we do not have to download the file each time we want to display it (Listing 5-6).

Listing 5-6. Download and store picture contents

```
let response = await axios.get(row.url, {responseType:
'arraybuffer'});
pictures[row.category] = Buffer.from (response.data).toString
('base64');
```

Each time we aim to change the picture to be displayed, we simply change the value of the image variable, and this is reflected on the display. The HTML file remains the same as previously.

Using setTimeout(), we ensure the pictures are downloaded every minute, so any change we make is not to be reflected instantly in the interface. All these changes are visible in the following code listing, where we place the full contents of the **app.js** file (Listing 5-7).

Listing 5-7. The application that retrieves pictures from Google Drive

```
const Vue = require ('vue/dist/vue.common.js');
const child_process = require ('child_process');
const fs = require ('fs-extra');
const axios = require ('axios');
const path = require ('path');

const azureHeader = {'Content-Type': 'application/octet-stream',
  'Ocp-Apim-Subscription-Key': '<your_key>'};
const azureURL = 'https://westcentralus.api.cognitive.
microsoft.com/face/v1.0/detect?returnFaceAttributes=gender';
```

```
const credentials = require ('./credentials.json');

var GoogleSpreadsheet = require('google-spreadsheet');

var doc = new GoogleSpreadsheet('<file_id>');

let pictures = {};

let app = new Vue ({
    el: '#app',
    data(){
        return {
                image:"
        };
    },
  async created() {
    doc.useServiceAccountAuth(credentials, ()=>{
        let getPictures = ()=>{
            doc.getRows(1, async (err, rows)=>{
                if (!err){
                    for (let row of rows){
                        try{
                            let response = await axios.get
                            (row.url, {responseType:
                            'arraybuffer'});
                            pictures[row.category] =
                            Buffer.from (response.data).
                            toString('base64');
                        }
                        catch (err){
                            console.log (err);
                        }
                    }
```

```
                        this.image = pictures.male;
                }
            });
            setInterval (getPictures, 60000);
        };
        getPictures();
    });
    let takePicture = async ()=>{
        try{
            let command = 'raspistill -o /home/pi/image';
              await child_process.exec (command);
            let imageBuffer = await fs.readFile ('/home/pi/
            image');
            let result = await axios.post (azureURL,
            imageBuffer, {headers:azureHeader});
            if (result.data.length > 0 && result.data[0].
            faceAttributes.gender){
                this.image = pictures[result.data[0].
                faceAttributes.gender];
            }
            setTimeout(takePicture, 15000);
        }
        catch(err){
            console.log (err);
        }
    };
    takePicture ();
  }
});
```

Connect USB Camera

While the Raspberry Pi camera module is suitable for prototyping IoT systems like the one presented earlier, its characteristics are limited, and you will most probably not see it integrated into any production devices. Many solutions existing on the market rely on different types of cameras that are connected via USB or other standard connectors. This way, it is easier to change the camera in case it gets damaged or needs to be upgraded.

To bring this example closer to a production system, we replace the Raspberry Pi camera module with a webcam that connects over USB. In this case, the first step after plugging in the camera is to install a CLI tool that enables us to control it. To achieve this, we need to open a shell and type sudo apt-get install fswebcam.

fswebcam is a CLI application available for Debian Linux distributions (Raspbian is also a Debian distribution) used to capture and manipulate pictures from various sources. It supports a wide array of operations such as capturing JPEG or PNG images, set image resolution, flip or crop pictures, and so on.

For this chapter, we use only the capture images capability, which translates to executing the following command: fswebcam/home/pi/img.jpg. This generates a new image file taken with the webcam connected to the Raspberry Pi.

Note   The picture contains a banner displaying the date and time it was taken. To generate the file without the banner, add the --no-banner option to the command: fswebcam --no-banner /home/ pi/img.jpg.

To actually integrate the fswebcam module in the application, we simply need to replace the command executed using the `child_process` module (Listing 5-8).

Listing 5-8. Take pictures using the webcam

```
child_process.execSync ('fswebcam --no-banner /home/pi/img.jpg');
```

Monitor the Environment

So far, the system we have built takes a picture every 15 seconds and sends it to the web service to be analyzed. This can result in unnecessary processing, as there might be moments when there is nobody around the display. In this context, the final step in building a complete and efficient solution is to add a motion sensor that tells us if there are people around.

The motion sensor is designed to detect presence in its proximity. Similarly to radars, these sensors usually emit lights, sounds, or microwaves into the environment and detect the amount and the time in which the emitted energy is returned to the source. Based on this, they can sense if there is anybody or anything around.

For our prototype, we use a PIR sensor,[4] which is one of the most accessible and easy-to-use motion sensors. Its name stands for *passive infrared*, which means that it contains a pyroelectric sensor that detects the level of *infrared radiation (IR)*. To detect motion, the sensor contains two lenses that are sensitive to the IR. In the idle state, the radiation detected by both lenses is the same, but when a person or an animal moves around, as they generate heat, the two lenses detect a different IR value, telling us that there is somebody in the proximity.

---

[4]https://thepihut.com/products/pir-infrared-motion-sensor-hc-sr501

Although it is a complex peripheral, connecting and reading data from a PIR sensor is a simple operation. The sensor has three legs, one that needs to be connected to the ground, one that is connected to the 5V pin, and another one that needs to be connected to a GPIO pin (Figure 5-14). To tell if there is somebody around or not, we read the value on the GPIO pin, and if it is equal to one, that means that motion was detected. Otherwise, the reading returns zero.

Caution   The sensor we use, HC-SR501, is designed to output 3.3V, the same voltage that the Raspberry Pi works with. When connected to 5V, other sensors might output 5V, which will fry the Raspberry Pi. When buying a presence sensor, make sure you read the datasheet, and the output voltage is 3.3V.

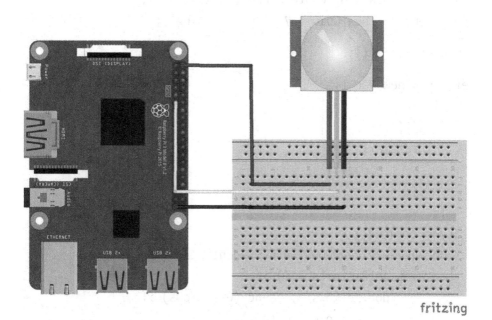

Figure 5-14. *PIR connection schematic*

Listing 5-9. PIR sensor integrated in app.js

```
const Vue = require ('vue/dist/vue.common.js');
const child_process = require ('child_process');
const fs = require ('fs-extra');
const axios = require ('axios');
const path = require ('path');
const Gpio = require ('onoff').Gpio;
const GoogleSpreadsheet = require('google-spreadsheet');

const azureHeader = {'Content-Type': 'application/octet-stream',
 'Ocp-Apim-Subscription-Key': '<your_key>'};
const azureURL = 'https://westcentralus.api.cognitive.
microsoft.com/face/v1.0/detect?returnFaceAttributes=gender';
const credentials = require ('./credentials.json');
const doc = new GoogleSpreadsheet('<file_id>');
const sensor = new Gpio (17, 'in', 'rising');

let pictures = {};

let app = new Vue ({
    el: '#app',
    data(){
        return {
                image:"
        };
    },
  async created() {
    doc.useServiceAccountAuth(credentials, ()=>{
        let getPictures = ()=>{
            doc.getRows(1, async (err, rows)=>{
                console.log (err);
```

```
        if (!err){
            for (let row of rows){
                try{
                    let response = await axios.
                    get(row.url, {responseType:
                    'arraybuffer'});
                    pictures[row.category] =
                    Buffer.from (response.data).
                    toString('base64');
                }
                catch (err){
                    console.log (err);
                }
            }
            this.image = pictures.male;
        }
    });
    setInterval (getPictures, 60000);
};
getPictures();
});
start = Date.now();
sensor.watch (async (err, value)=>{
    if (!err && (Date.now()-start)/1000 > 10){
        start = Date.now();
        try{
            let command = 'raspistill -o /home/pi/image';
            await child_process.exec (command);
            let imageBuffer = await fs.readFile ('/home/pi/
            image');
```

```
                let result = await axios.post (azureURL,
                imageBuffer, {headers:azureHeader});
                if (result.data.length > 0 && result.data[0].
                faceAttributes.gender){
                    this.image = pictures[result.data[0].
                    faceAttributes.gender];
                }
            }
            catch(err){
                console.log (err);
            }
        }
    });
  }
});
```

To be computationally efficient, the system we desire to obtain should take and process pictures only when there are people present. We also need to ensure one picture stays on the screen long enough so it is visible. Thus, we decided not to change the image faster than once per minute (Listing 5-9).

To achieve this behavior, we first imported the onoff module and initialized the sensor variable on pin 17. We also specified the pin to act as input. The third parameter, 'rising', specifies that an interrupt should be generated each time the value on the GPIO changes from zero to one. In our case, this happens when the sensor detects movement.

Since the interrupt is registered, once the application is loaded, we can call the watch() function and pass as parameter the callback function. The callback function is called each time a rising edge is detected. Inside the callback function we do the same actions as previously, but only if the time since the last picture change is longer than one minute. To do this, we declare the global variable, start, where we store the date when a picture is taken.

Caution   Make sure onoff is installed on the system. You can check its status and install it with the Package Manager of Wyliodrin STUDIO.

Summary

In this chapter, we have built a smart advertising system by connecting a camera module to the Raspberry Pi.

To analyze the images we captured, we used *Microsoft Cognitive Services*, which are suited to extract information about people from pictures. For other applications, where additional details need to be extracted, we can use other web services. Considering the computing capabilities that the Raspberry Pi has, some of the services available can be installed on the device, so there is no Internet connection required (e.g., openALPR[5]).

We also integrated the Google Drive service so we can remotely update the content being displayed. To interact with the service, we imported the google-spreadsheet module. However, you can also follow the instructions[6] that Google provides and integrate the service into the application via plain HTTP requests.

To make the system more efficient and adapted to the environment, we added a presence sensor, so we take pictures only when there are people around. This helps reduce processing power consumption, which is very important for an autonomous system.

---

[5]www.openalpr.com

[6]https://developers.google.com/drive/api/v3/about-sdk

To take the application to the next level and make it work as an actual smart advertising system, we recommend that you set the content updates once per day. Also, for a more precise system, we recommend you explore the cognitive services API and extract more information for the pictures you take. Also, you should take into account the characteristics of all the people in the pictures, not only one person.

CHAPTER 6

Smart Metering System Using an Industrial Server

Sensing and monitoring people, gadgets, and the environment are a key feature of any IoT system. A large number of sensors deployed in IoT systems have the task of collecting the appropriate information and then sending it up the IoT stack where extended storage and processing capabilities exist, as explained in Chapter 1. As a famous management saying goes, "you cannot manage what you do not measure." In the context of IoT system, predictive maintenance is an emerging technique that uses detailed data collected about commercial and industrial processes in order to estimate when breakdowns will occur and maintenance should be performed.

Examples include environment monitoring (e.g., biomonitoring of chemical compounds in cities, farms, roads, and parks), people monitoring (e.g., especially vulnerable people such as babies, children, and seniors), healthcare monitoring (e.g., wearables such as smartwatches), and industrial monitoring (e.g., status of industrial equipment or electrical energy consumption levels). In many commercial and industrial IoT systems, *energy monitoring and targeting (M&T)* is a crucial task for cost reduction but also environmental concerns especially given the worries about the negative effects of global warming. Energy M&T allows us to track

© Ioana Culic; Alexandru Radovici; Cristian Rusu 2020
I. Culic et al., *Commercial and Industrial Internet of Things Applications with the Raspberry Pi*,
https://doi.org/10.1007/978-1-4842-5296-3_6

energy consumption in real time, identify areas or periods of anomalous consumption, predict future consumption patterns, and manage overall consumption (e.g., the modern energy markets which include renewable energy sources). The ultimate goal of energy M&T is to improve the energy efficiency of IoT systems.

Also, so far, we have created several simple applications in order to get used to working with the Raspberry Pi. All the projects we have created so far are monolithic, which means that the software we wrote consists of one major component. The user interface, the control system (access of the pins), and the Internet connection were tightly coupled together. While this approach has the advantage of speed and efficiency, it also has some significant disadvantages. If one piece fails (due to a hardware or software error), the whole system fails and stops running. It is then challenging to modify one of the parts. Say we want to make a new user interface or use a different web monitoring system. This becomes increasingly difficult. We will have to modify all the components to work with the new part. This is not the desired behavior when it comes to an industrial project.

In this chapter, we aim to build an industrial system that monitors the power consumption. This complex application consists of multiple modules that are interconnected via the OPC Unified Architecture (UA).

Industrial Applications Architecture

Any standard industrial software is built using decoupled components. Figure 6-1 describes the architecture of such a system. Ideally, each component is a separate piece of software, running independently. If one of them fails, it does not bring down the whole system. If a component has to be replaced, all the others remain untouched; the only code that is being modified is the targeted component itself. To achieve this, all of the components need to communicate with each other using a standard language, usually called interface or protocol.

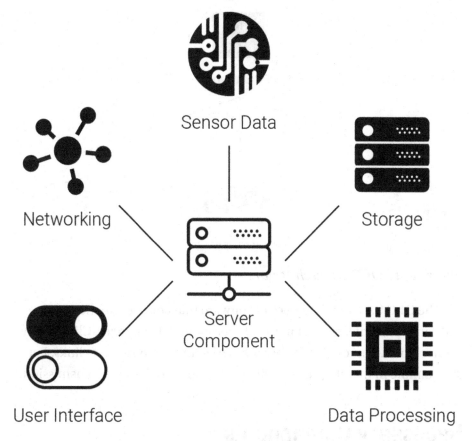

Figure 6-1. Industrial applications architecture

An example of such a language or protocol is the *Open Platform Communication – Unified Architecture* (OPC UA). OPC UA allows the interconnection of several components that need to communicate to each other and exchange data. The general architecture of an OPC UA system consists of a server and several clients. The server is used just like a database with several specific features. Its purpose is to store data and serve it to the clients that connect to it. Data is organized in a hierarchical way (similar to the computer's file system). It has folders that consist of other subfolders and properties. Figure 6-2 describes an OPC UA Server example.

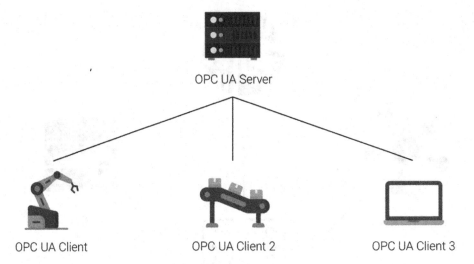

Figure 6-2. *OPC UA architecture*

The OPC UA client is a piece of software that connects to the server and can read, write, and get notifications about data changes. Clients may connect to the server via the network, serial lines, or other data links. For the example in this chapter, we will use the network for data transmission.

Necessary Components

The software that we will design and implement is a smart plug power meter for a smart house. For this, we will use

- One Raspberry Pi connected to Wyliodrin STUDIO.

- TP-Link HS110 Smart Wi-Fi Plug[1].

- Raspberry Pi Touch Display or HDMI Display.

---

[1]www.kasasmart.com/us/products/smart-plugs/kasa-smart-plug-energy-monitoring-hs110

Note   You may use any other smart power plug. The only
requirement is that it should have some open API that you can use
to control it. Some of the smart power plugs only work with their
specific phone apps and cloud systems.

The Smart Power Plug Interface

The system's architecture is illustrated in Figure 6-3. Its main component is
the OPC UA Server, which stores all the system's data. The system has three
major components: one that interacts with the smart power plug, one that
connects the device to the Internet, and a component that displays the
information to the user.

Note   In this system, the only components that have to be present
are the server and the power plug interface. All the others may be
missing, and the system still works.

The purpose of the smart power plug interface is to control the smart
power plug, switch it on and off, and read the power metrics (power,
current, and voltage).

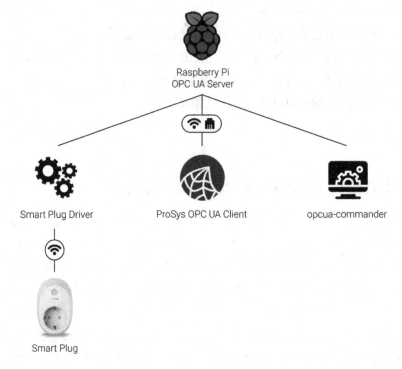

Figure 6-3. *Smart plug system architecture*

We use a TP-Link HS110 Smart Power Plug. We have chosen this model as it can be purchased at a reasonable price, and it is easy to find. Most important, though, the plug may be controlled using a small Python script.

The next step is to configure the power plug to connect to the local Wi-Fi network so we can then control and read data from it. The configuration process can be done in two ways, either by using the Kasa app or by using a Python application.

Set Up the HS110 Smart Power Plug Using the Kasa App

The first step is to set up the power plug. The easiest way is to download the TP-Link's Kasa phone app and set it up using your mobile device. The app is available for iOS and Android from their respective app stores. From the app, connect the power plugs to your Wi-Fi network following the instructions provided. The steps should be the following:

1. The power plug provides a small Wi-Fi access point that your phone can connect to; connect your phone to the plug's Wi-Fi.

2. Run the Kasa app; it should discover the power plug.

3. Using the app, provide your Wi-Fi network credentials to the power plug.

4. The power plug disconnects your phone from its Wi-Fi network and connects to the provided Wi-Fi network.

5. Write down the power plug's new IP address (from the app or your Wi-Fi router); the MAC address of the power plug should be similar to 50:c7:bf:0b:37:fd.

Set Up the HS110 Smart Power Plug Using the Python SDK

Setting up the smart power plug using the app requires you to sign up to a cloud system. If you do not want to do this, you can set up the HS110 power plug using the Python SDK. For this, you need a computer that has Python installed and is able to connect to a Wi-Fi network. You can also use a Raspberry Pi for this.

Note We use the Raspberry Pi to set up the power plug. You can follow the same steps using a computer.

The first item on the list is to connect to the power plug. For this, insert the power plug into a power socket, then press and hold the small button located on the top of the power plug until the LED display next to the Wi-Fi sign turns orange. This means the power plug starts an access point (AP) with the SSID TP-Link_Smart Plug_XXXX where XXXX is replaced by the last digits of the MAC address of the power plug. This is unique to every power plug and is located on the back of the power plug.

Using Wyliodrin STUDIO's Network Manager located in the device menu, connect the Raspberry Pi to the Wi-Fi network of the power plug, as shown in Figure 6-4. Please note that the power plug's Wi-Fi network has no password.

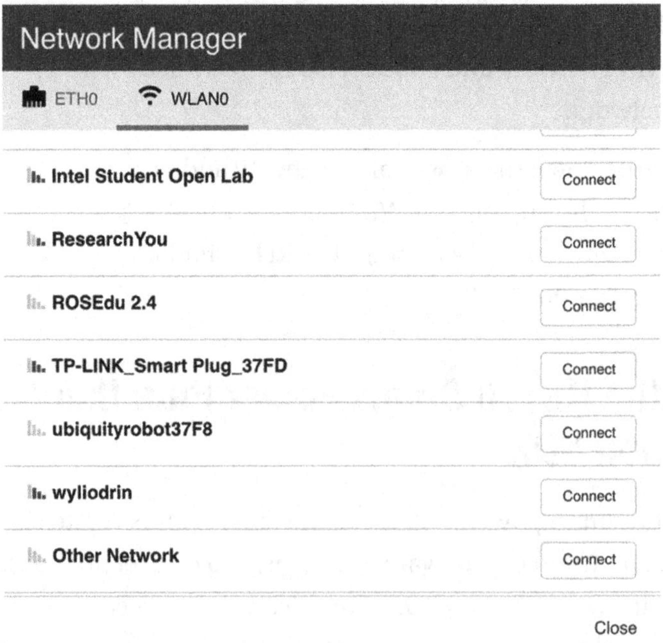

Network Manager	
ETH0 **WLAN0**	
Intel Student Open Lab	Connect
ResearchYou	Connect
ROSEdu 2.4	Connect
TP-LINK_Smart Plug_37FD	Connect
ubiquityrobot37F8	Connect
wyliodrin	Connect
Other Network	Connect

Close

Figure 6-4. *Raspberry Pi Network Manager*

Caution   Before connecting the Raspberry Pi to the power plug's Wi-Fi network, make sure that the Raspberry Pi is connected to a wired network; otherwise, you lose connection to the Raspberry Pi.

To set up the power plug's Wi-Fi credentials so that it can connect to your Wi-Fi network, we use the same Raspberry Pi that runs the system. First, we need to open the SHELL tab in Wyliodrin STUDIO. In the shell, we clone the HS110 Python SDK repository using: git clone https:// github.com/softScheck/tplink-smartplug.

Inside the resulting folder, we can find a file titled **tplink_smartplug. py**. This file is a command-line utility that sends commands to the power plug. To use it, we have to run python tplink_smartplug, followed by several parameters. The most important available parameters are listed in Table 6-1.

Table 6-1. *HS110 command-line interface parameters*

Parameter	Required	Description
-t IP_ADDRESS	Yes	Specify the IP address of the power plug
-c COMMAND	No	Send a command to the power plug, used for simple commands, usually queries
--json JSON_ COMMAND	No	Send a command in JSON format to the power plug, used for commands that have a set of parameters, usually settings

The first parameter that we have to use is -t. This allows us to specify the IP address of the smart plug. While the power plug is being set up and the Raspberry Pi is connected to its Wi-Fi network, the IP address is 192.168.0.1.

The first command that we run in the shell is a query command to check if the power plug receives commands: `python tplink_smartplug.py -t 102.168.0.1 -c info`.

This should display the JSON message in Listing 6-1.

Listing 6-1. Details about the power plug in JSON format

```
Sent:      {"system":{"get_sysinfo":{}}}
Received:  {"system":{"get_sysinfo":{"err_code":0, "sw_
ver":"1.1.0 Build 160503 Rel.144605", "hw_ver":"1.0",
"type":"IOT.SMARTPLUGSWITCH", "model":"HS110(EU)",
"mac":"50:C7:BF:0B:37:FD", "deviceId":"8006A31AB763DAFF6C620B8
19B8A853A17ACD19C","hwId":"45E29DA8382494D2E82688B52A0B2EB5",
"fwId":"B78BB2C0C8C2A9D31A75E0CD71430A5F", "oemId":"3D341ECE3
02C0642C99E31CE2430544B", "alias":"TP-LINK_Smart Plug_37FD",
"dev_name":"Wi-Fi Smart Plug With Energy Monitoring",
"icon_hash":"", "relay_state":1, "on_time":19576, "active_
mode":"none", "feature":"TIM:ENE", "updating":0, "led_off":0,
"latitude":0, "longitude":0}}}
```

Now that the command line is able to connect to the power plug, we can set up the Wi-Fi network. We run the command in Listing 6-2 using the -j parameter.

Listing 6-2. Connect the power plug to the Wi-Fi network

```
python tplink_smartplug.py -t 192.168.0.1 -j '{"netif":{"set_st
ainfo":{"ssid":"SSID","password":"PASSWORD","key_type":3}}}'
```

Note   Replace SSID and PASSWORD with your wireless network's SSID and password.

After running the command, you should see a message like the one in Listing 6-3.

Listing 6-3. Wi-Fi setup response

```
Sent:     {"netif":{"set_stainfo":{"ssid":"your_ssid",
"password":"your_password","key_type":3}}}
Received: {"netif":{"set_stainfo":{"mac":"51:A8:BF:0B:37:AD","
err_code":0}}}
```

If err_code is 0, then everything worked fine; the power plug tries to connect to your wireless network. If the command is successful, the power plug connects to your Wi-Fi network and disconnects the Raspberry Pi from the Wi-Fi. Now we can send commands to the power plug via our Wi-Fi network.

All we have to do now is to find out the power plug's IP address. For this, we install the arp-scan software using the following command line: sudo apt-get install arp-scan.

The tool that we just installed can be used to find out the IP address of the power plug. First, we have to know the Raspberry Pi's IP address and network mask. These are displayed in the *Network Manager* window. The Raspberry Pi that we use has two network interfaces, a wired one (eth0) and a wireless one (wlan0). As we used the Wi-Fi network to set up the power plug, the Raspberry Pi's main network connection is the wired one (eth0). All the information we need is shown in the ETH0 tab. You should see something similar to Figure 6-5.

Having all the data, we can run the network tool using the following syntax: sudo arp-scan IP_ADDRESS:NETWORK_MASK. With the settings shown in Figure 6-5, the command is sudo arp-scan 192.168.1.151:255.255.255.0.

Note   Your network settings might be different than the ones we have here; please update the command line according to your settings.

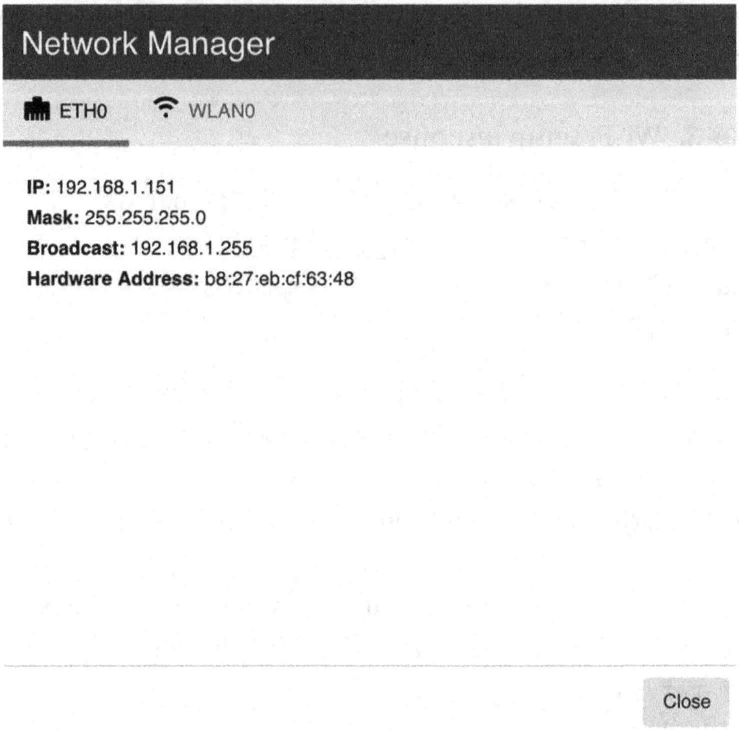

Network Manager

ETH0   WLAN0

IP: 192.168.1.151
Mask: 255.255.255.0
Broadcast: 192.168.1.255
Hardware Address: b8:27:eb:cf:63:48

Close

Figure 6-5. *Raspberry Pi wired network settings*

If the command is successful, you should see something similar to
Listing 6-4.

Listing 6-4. Network scan results

```
Starting arp-scan 1.9.5 with 256 hosts (https://github.com/
royhills/arp-scan)
192.168.1.1      10:7b:44:5b:24:0c   (Unknown)
192.168.1.121    c8:d3:ff:af:34:2b   Hewlett Packard
192.168.1.72     50:c7:bf:0b:37:fd   TP-LINK TECHNOLOGIES
                                     CO.,LTD.
192.168.1.191    18:66:da:05:b7:8c   Dell Inc.
192.168.1.84     b8:27:eb:af:65:63   Raspberry Pi Foundation
```

```
192.168.1.161    44:03:2c:ea:70:1d    (Unknown)
192.168.1.177    78:4f:43:77:58:db    (Unknown)
192.168.1.242    24:5e:be:03:4d:c5    QNAP Systems, Inc.
192.168.1.169    50:c7:bf:0b:38:17    TP-LINK TECHNOLOGIES
                                      CO.,LTD.
192.168.1.239    14:ab:c5:6f:aa:81    (Unknown)
```

Note   The list of addresses and devices that you see might be different.

By examining that list, we can see that we have two power plugs called TP-LINK TECHNOLOGIES CO.,LTD. To identify the one that we have just set up, we have to look at its MAC address displayed in the second column. The IP address that we are looking for is the one corresponding to the MAC address that is written on the power plug. In our example, the MAC address is 50:c7:bf:0b:37:fd and the IP address is 192.168.1.72.

Tip   The IP address is leased to the power plug by your wireless router. In most of the cases, as long as the plug stays connected, this address does not change. If you want to make sure it never changes, please set up your DHCP server on the router to always lease the same IP address to the power plug by associating the MAC address to the IP address. This process is called *assigning a static IP address*.

To make sure that everything works fine, let us run the following command one more time: python tplink_smartplug.py -t 192.168.1.72 -c info.

This should print in the shell all the information about the power plug. Everything is now in place.

Write the Power Plug Driver

Now that we have set up the HS110 power plug, we can move forward to building the control interface for it.

After setting up the power plug, you should have written down its IP address. This should never change.

Now let us write our interface. Using Wyliodrin STUDIO, please make a new *Node.js* project. The next step is to add the Python software that sends and receives commands from the power plug. For this, please go to *https://github.com/softScheck/tplink-smartplug* and download the file named **tplink_smartplug.py**. Make a folder called **driver** in your Wyliodrin STUDIO project and import the downloaded file there. Your project layout should look like the one in Figure 6-6.

Figure 6-6. *The project structure*

We now use Node.js to run that Python script. As the Python script was designed to be run by a user from a console and not from another application, it displays a little too much information on the screen. To solve this, we have to make a small change. Open the **tplink_smartplug.py** file and find the line similar to print "Sent:", cmd.

Comment this line by adding a # sign in front of it. The next line should be similar, just that instead of Sent it shows Received. Modify this line so that it writes print "Received: ", decrypt(data[4:]) or similar depending on the version of the script that you have. After the modifications are done, these two lines should look like in Listing 6-5.

Listing 6-5. tplink-smartplug.py lines changed

```
# print "Sent:        ", cmd
print decrypt(data[4:])
```

These changes to the script make it much easier to use from another program. Also, the modified version of the script writes on the screen only the response in JSON format. This format is straightforward to understand and manipulate from any Node.js application.

Now let us write a small Node.js library that is able to control the script. Create a new file called **tplink_smartplug.js**. This file's contents should look similar to Listing 6-6.

Listing 6-6. tplink_smartplug.js contents

```
const util = require('util');
const exec = util.promisify (require('child_process').exec);

async function tplinkSmartplug(deviceIp, command, data = {})
{
   let response = {};
   try
   {
       let js = await exec('python "' + __dirname + '/tplink_
       smartplug.py" -t ' + deviceIp + ' -c ' + command);
       response = JSON.parse(js.stdout);
   }
```

```javascript
    catch (e)
    {
        console.error('Error for ' + deviceIp + ', command ' +
        command + ', (' + e.message + ')');
    }
    return response;
}

async function readEnergy (deviceIp)
{
    let energy = {};
    let js = await tplinkSmartplug (deviceIp, 'energy');
    if (js.emeter && js.emeter.get_realtime && js.emeter.get_
    realtime.err_code === 0)
    {
        energy = js.emeter.get_realtime;
    }
    return energy;
}

async function on(deviceIp)
{
    return tplinkSmartplug(deviceIp, 'on');
}

async function off(deviceIp)
{
    return tplinkSmartplug(deviceIp, 'off');
}

module.exports.on = on;
module.exports.off = off;
module.exports.readEnergy = readEnergy;
```

Let us take every line and explain it in detail. First, we have to import the `child_process` library. This allows us to run commands from Node.js. We need this library as we have to run the Python script. This library has been part of Node.js since its beginnings, so its API is with callback functions. As the new versions of Node.js allow the use of `async` and `await`, we use the `util` library to adapt the functions from `child_process` to use this new way of programming. The function that we need from `util` is `promisify`.

One of the functions that allow us to run a command from Node.js is `exec()`. We import that function from `child_process` and use `promisify` to transform it so that it can be used with `async` and `await`.

Next, we designed a function named `tplinkSmartplug()` whose purpose is to send a command to the smart plug (using the Python script) and return a Node.js object with the information that is sent back by the power plug. The function takes two arguments: `deviceIP`, which is the IP address of the desired power plug, and `command`, a string with the command to be sent. As you can see, we create an empty response object. This object is replaced by the actual response or, if an error occurs, it returns empty.

The `exec()` function receives only one parameter, a string with the shell command to run. It starts with `python` followed by the Python script, `-t`, and the `deviceIp` parameter, and after that by `-c` and the command. The `__dirname` variable represents the folder where the current Node.js script (**tplink_smartplug.js**) is placed. As this is the same folder as the Python script to be run, we just add to it `./tplink_smartplug.py`.

> **Note**   The exec function is enclosed in a `try` - `catch` structure.
> This is a good idea as the commands that run outside Node.js might
> fail for several reasons, and we do not want this to stop our script.

> **Caution**   The quotes around `'python "'` + `__dirname` +
> `'/tplink_smartplug.py" -t '` are important. If your project
> name has a space in it and the quotes are missing, `exec()` shows
> an error.

If `exec()` is successful, a JSON string should be returned and stored in
the `js` variable. We can now parse it to transform it into a JavaScript object
and return it. If there is an error, the `catch` part is executed where an error
is printed, and the empty result is returned.

Next we define three functions:

- `readEnergy()` – Returns an object with the power
  consumption data

- `on()` – Switches the power plug on

- `off()` – Switches the power plug off

All that is left to do is to export the functions so they can be used from a
file that is going to import our script.

Now let us test our Node.js power plug script. In the **main.js** file of your
project, write the lines in Listing 6-7.

Listing 6-7. Test the power plug control script

```
let smartpower = require ('./driver/tplink_smartplug.js');
smartpower.on ('192.168.1.72');
```

Run the project. If the power plug switches on, the script is working
properly. The driver is not yet complete; we will finish it later.

The OPC UA Server

The main component of our system is the OPC UA Server. To build it, we use a Node.js library called node-opcua. This library provides developers with the ability to easily write OPC UA Servers and clients. For the server, the heavy lifting is done by the library: setting up the actual server, receiving connections from clients, and storing the actual data. The developer is responsible for the data model, which means describing the actual data that is stored inside the server.

Using node-opcua, developers have two ways of describing the data model: using Node.js source code or via a standard XML file. We use the first option, but instead of us writing the source code, we use Wyliodrin STUDIO's visual OPC UA data model editor.

Note   The OPC UA standard describes a standard way of setting up the data model using XML files. The downside is that this XML way is more complicated and adds too much overhead to our system.

First, let us add a folder called **server** to our project. This is where we store all the files related to the OPC UA. In this folder, we create a file **server.opcuamodel**. Please note that you may call the file with any other name as long as the extension is **opcuamodel**. Now when you select the file, Wyliodrin STUDIO shows you a visual interface where you can design the data model. This interface is presented in Figure 6-7. As you can see in the figure, the visual language has two blocks: OPC UA Folder and OPC UA Variable. We described before the OPC UA data structure as being a hierarchical one. It actually consists of two elements: folders and variables.

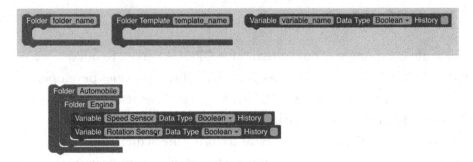

Figure 6-7. *Wyliodrin STUDIO visual OPC UA data model editor*

Folders are used to group several folders and variables. Variables are the actual data storage items. Each variable has several parameters, the most important being: the name, the ID, the data type, and whether or not it stores historical data. Let us take them one by one.

The name of the variable is what you, the developer or administrator of the system, see in an OPC UA explorer software. This is a program similar to the file explorer.

The ID of the variable is what you, as a developer, need to know when accessing the server. The ID has the following format: ns=<number>;s=<text>. The first part, ns=<number>, is the part that represents the namespace (ns). This is always a number. The OPC UA separates the data into several namespaces. For this project (and for all the other projects that we build), we use only namespace number 1. The second part, s=<text>, is the actual ID. It can be any text.

Note   The Wyliodrin STUDIO visual model editor generates for each variable the following ID: ns=1;s=</path/to/variable>. For instance, if we have a folder named **Sensors** that has a subfolder called **Light** that contains a variable named diningRoom, the ID is: ns=1;/Sensors/Light/diningRoom.

The data type parameter specifies the data type of the stored variable. Table 6-2 describes the main data types that the OPC UA standard provides.

Table 6-2. *OPC UA data types*

Name	Data Type Description
Boolean	A value that may be either *true* or *false*.
Byte	An unsigned number stored on 8 bits (0 to 255).
ByteString	An array of bytes.
DataValue	A value together with a status and a timestamp.
DateTime	Stores the date and time.
Double	A floating-point number using the IEEE 754 on 64 bits.
Float	A floating-point number using the IEEE 754 on 32 bits.
GUID	A global unique ID (same as UUID).
Int16	A number using 16 bits (-32768 to 32767).
Int32	A number using 32 bits (-2147483648 to 2147483647).
Int64	A number using 64 bits (-9223372036854775808 to 9223372036854775807).
LocalizedText	A text together with the locale information.
NodeId	A value that stores another OPC UA variable ID (*ns=<number>;s=<text>* or *ns=<number>;id=<number>*).
QualifiedName	A name together with a namespace name.
SByte	A value that stores a signed number using 8 bits (-128 to 127).
String	A text.
UInt16	An unsigned number using 16 bits (0 to 65 535).
UInt32	An unsigned number using 32 bits (0 to 4294967295).

(continued)

Table 6-2. (*continued*)

Name	Data Type Description
UInt64	An unsigned number using 64 bits (0 and 18446744073709551615).
Variant	The value description of another variable.
XmlElement	An XML element.

Another important parameter is whether or not to keep historical data. This instructs the server to keep or not several data points when the value changes, enabling clients to read the previous values of the variable.

OPC UA Variables

It is important to say a few words about the OPC UA variables. When storing such a variable, it is composed of several fields:

- Value – The actual value that is stored.

- Type – The data type of the value that is stored.

- Timestamps – The date and time when the value has been modified.

- History – Optionally keep a list of previous values.

- Status code – The status of the value; this is a property that adds semantic information to the value. Table 6-3 presents some of the possible status codes.

Table 6-3. *Available OPC UA status codes for values*

Status Code	Description
Good	The value is normal.
Bad	The value has an error.
GoodLocalOverride	The value has been overwritten.
Uncertain	The value is uncertain or unknown.
GoodEdited	The value is not the original; it has been modified by the server.

The OPC UA Server

The first step in building our server is to set up the data model. Open the **server.opcuamodel** file, drag an OPC UA Folder block, and name it SmartPower. Inside, drag another OPC UA Folder block and name it SmartPlug1. Inside this block, drag an OPC UA Variable block and name it power. This is the value that indicates whether the power plug is on or off. Set the data type of this variable to Boolean, then drag another OPC UA Folder block and name it Energy. This folder has three variables that hold the power consumption values. The data model should be similar to the one presented in Figure 6-8.

While you are dragging and dropping blocks, the editor is writing the Node.js source code for you. If you click the *Show Source* button, you are able to see how it looks like. Moreover, the source code is saved in a file called **server.opcuamodel.js** placed in the same folder as the model file (in our case **server**). You can also open that file to see the code.

Caution   You may edit the source code generated for the model, but please keep in mind that it will be overwritten any time you open and modify the model using the visual editor.

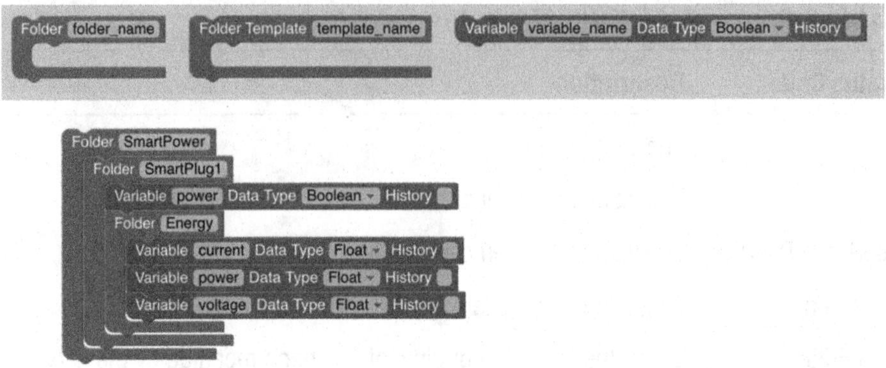

Figure 6-8. *The OPC UA data model for the smart power plug*

Now that we have created the data model, let us create the server. We make a new file called **index.js** in the **server** folder and write in it the file the code displayed in Listing 6-8.

Listing 6-8. The index.js file contents

```
const opcua = require('node-opcua');

function loadSettings (server)
{
    require ('./server.opcuamodel.js')(server);
}

async function run ()
{
    const server = new opcua.OPCUAServer({
        alternateHostname: ['localhost', '192.168.1.151'],
        port: 4840, // the port of the listening //socket of the
        server
        resourcePath: '/UA/SmartPlugsServer',  //this path will
        be added to the endpoint //resource name
```

```
    buildInfo : {
        productName: 'SmartPlugs Server',
        buildNumber: '7658',
        buildDate: new Date()
    }
});

try
{
    await server.start ();
    loadSettings (server);

    console.log ('Server started at '+server.endpoints[0].
    endpointDescriptions()[0].endpointUrl);
}
catch (e)
{
    console.error ('Server error: '+e.message);
}
}

run ();
```

The first step is to load the node-opcua library. This allows us to create an OPC UA Server and client. The actions that we have to take to start a server are to set up the server properties and load the data model. As node-opcua is able to work with `await` and `async`, we wrap the code in an `async` function, called run(). Our main program just runs this function (the last line of Listing 6-8).

Inside the run() function, we set the server properties and load the model. First, we create an OPCUAServer object that represents the server. Among the properties of the object, we have

- port – The port number that the server listens on; the default value for OPC UA is 4840.

- alternativeHostname – All the hostnames that can be used to connect to the server; we add here localhost and the Raspberry Pi's IP address (as we try to connect from the computer to the Raspberry Pi).

- resourcePath – This is the *path to the server resources*, the string that follows the hostname.

- buildInfo – This is the information about the server; you can write any values here. In this example, we have set the name of the server to Smart PowerPlugs, the date to the current date, and the build to the first version.

Note   The OPC UA Server uses the Raspberry Pi's hostname for accepting connections. As this hostname might change, we suggest adding localhost as this is always valid. Moreover, if you have some components connecting to the server from outside the Raspberry Pi, make sure you add the Raspberry Pi's IP address and that this address is not changed.

Now we can start the server using the server.start() function. This function is an asynchronous one, so we need to use the await keyword.

The last action that we take is to load the model. We have created a wrapper function called loadModel() that loads the JavaScript file generated by the OPC UA visual editor. This function requires the server object as an argument and passes it to the JavaScript file containing the model that is loaded.

Now that we have the server, we run it to make sure that the data model is correct and the server behaves as expected. For this, we import the server files in the main project: replace the contents of the **main.js** file with the following: `require ('./server');`

Note   As you can see, we are importing a folder instead of a file. Node.js imports the **index.js** file that is placed inside the folder. This has the same effect as writing require (`'./server/index.js'`);

Now we can run the project. You should see some text popping up in the console and after some time a line stating *Server started at opc.tcp:// raspberrypi:4840/UA/SmartPlugsServer*. This means that the server is up and running.

Note   It takes a few seconds to start the server, do not panic if it takes a little bit longer.

To see the server data model, we need to use an OPC UA explorer. There are two options available: *opcua-commander,* a text mode explorer that we are able to run from the Raspberry Pi, and *ProSys OPC UA Client* that runs on your computer and has a graphical user interface. We will try both of them.

OPC UA Commander

The *opcua-commander* software runs on the Raspberry Pi. To install it, we go to the *Package Manager* in the board menu, select Node.js, and install the *opcua-commander* library.

Note   It takes a few minutes to install *opcua-commander*.

Once the library is installed, we are able to use it from the shell. We select the SHELL tab in Wyliodrin STUDIO, press any key to see the prompt, and run the command: `opcua-commander -e opc.tcp://raspberrypi:4840/UA/SmartPlugsServer`.

Note   The `-e` parameter for `opcua-commander` defines the endpoint for the server to connect to. Please use the same address that was printed by the server in the console.

After connecting, `opcua-commander` displays a text user interface with the server data. The interface is similar to the one presented in Figure 6-9. On the left side, we can see the data hierarchy. This should display three main folders: *Objects*, *Types*, and *Views*. If we select *Objects* and press *Enter* or *Right Arrow,* we can open it, and we should see two subfolders: *Server* and *1:SmartPower*.

Note   The `1:` in front of the folder and variables names is due to the fact that these objects are part of namespace number 1.

Figure 6-9. *OPC UA Commander*

ProSys OPC UA Client

Another tool that we can use to explore the OPC UA Server is *ProSys OPC UA Client*.[2] This tool is easier to use than `opcua-commander` but requires to be run on a computer. Please download and start ProSys OPC UA Client. At the top of the window, there is an address bar. We fill the address with the endpoint of the OPC UA Server. Please make sure to replace `raspberry` with the IP address of the Raspberry Pi.

---

[2]https://downloads.prosysopc.com/opc-ua-client-downloads.php

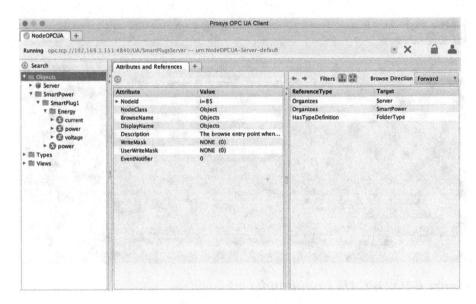

Figure 6-10. *The ProSys OPC UA Client connected to the server*

Tip   The IP address of the Raspberry Pi can be found using the *Network Manager*.

If we click the right arrow next to the address bar, after a few seconds, a small popup appears asking about the connection setup. We can select the value *None* for both *Security Mode* and *Security Policy*. After a few seconds, you should see something similar to Figure 6-10.

The left panel of *ProSys OPC UA Client* displays the server data hierarchy. You should see the folders and variables from the model. If you select any value, you see its properties in the *Attributes* and *References* tab. The main property is value, showing the actual value.

The Smart Power Plug Driver

The following step in this project is to connect the smart power plug to the
OPC UA Server. To do this, we get back to our power plug interface that is
stored in the **driver** folder. The steps that we need to take are the following:
connect to the OPC UA Server, request the power consumption values
from the power plug to monitor the power value, and turn the power plug
on and off depending on the value.

We first need to create a new file called **index.js** inside the **driver**
folder. There, we write the lines of code in Listing 6-9.

Listing 6-9. Index.js contents

```
const opcua = require("node-opcua")
const client = opcua.OPCUAClient.create();

async function run ()
{
    try
    {
        await client.connect ('opc.tcp://localhost:4840/UA/
        SmartPlugsServer');
        const session = await client.createSession();
        console.log ('SmartPlug connected to Server');
        const subscription= opcua.ClientSubscription.
        create(session,{
            requestedPublishingInterval: 1000,
            requestedLifetimeCount: 10,
            requestedMaxKeepAliveCount: 2,
            maxNotificationsPerPublish: 10,
            publishingEnabled: true,
            priority: 10
        });
```

```
        subscription.on("started", ()=>{
            console.log ('SmartPlug subscribed to server');
        });

    }
    catch (e)
    {
        console.error ('OPC UA error '+e.message);
    }
}

run ();
```

First, we import the node-opcua library and create an OPCUAClient object. This object allows us to connect to the OPC UA Server. As the library enables the use of async and await, we wrap the whole file in an async function called run(). Now that we have an OPC UA client, let us connect to the server. As the server and the client run on the Raspberry Pi, we can use the endpoint that the server prints out when it starts.

Note   For the endpoint, you can use either the hostname or localhost.

If the connection is successful, we have to set up a session. Each connection can have multiple sessions. For this example, we need only one. The session is created using createSession().

Write the Energy Values

After we create a session, we can read and write OPC UA Server variables. We use this to write the energy values read from the power plug. For this, we use the readEnergy() function that we have created for the power plug interface. For this, we have to import the power plug library, so we place the lines in Listing 6-10 after the node-opcua import.

Listing 6-10. Import the power plug interface

```
const smart = require ('./tplink_smartplug.js');
const DEVICE_IP = '192.168.1.72';
```

The `smart` variable represents the power plug interface and the `DEVICE_IP` is the IP address of the power plug.

Note   The IP address of you power plug might be different.

We set up a timer that reads the energy values from the power plug every 500ms and writes them to the OPC UA Server. At the bottom of the `run()` function, we add the lines in Listing 6-11.

Listing 6-11. Write OPC UA energy values

```
setInterval (async () => {
        let energy = await smart.readEnergy (DEVICE_IP);
        if (energy.err_code === 0)
        {
            try
            {
                await session.writeSingleNode ('ns=1;s=/
                SmartPower/SmartPlug1/Energy/current', new
                opcua.Variant ({
                    dataType: opcua.DataType.Float,
                    value: parseFloat (energy.current)
                }));
```

```
                    await session.writeSingleNode ('ns=1;s=/
                    SmartPower/SmartPlug1/Energy/voltage', new
                    opcua.Variant ({
                        dataType: opcua.DataType.Float,
                        value: parseFloat (energy.voltage)
                    }));
                    await session.writeSingleNode ('ns=1;s=/
                    SmartPower/SmartPlug1/Energy/power', new
                    opcua.Variant ({
                        dataType: opcua.DataType.Float,
                        value: parseFloat (energy.power)
                    }));
                }
                catch (e)
                {
                    console.error ('OPC UA server write error
                    '+e.message);
                }
            }
        }
    }, 500);
```

Every 500ms, the driver reads the energy values from the power plug
using the readEnergy() function. If the read is successful, the returned
object has a property called err_code set to 0. We check for that value, and
if it is 0, we write the values to the OPC UA Server. The function that writes
to the server is called writeSingleNode(). This allows us to write one
single value to one node. We also have to take into account what happens
if there is an error. For example, if the power plug disconnects from the
Wi-Fi network, we should report this as *Bad values* to the OPC UA Server.
To do this, we add an else branch to the error checking (Listing 6-12).

Listing 6-12. Add error checking

```
setInterval (async () => {
        try
        {
            let energy = await smart.readEnergy (DEVICE_IP);
            if (energy.err_code === 0)
            {
                await session.writeSingleNode ('ns=1;s=/
                SmartPower/SmartPlug1/Energy/current', new
                opcua.Variant ({
                    dataType: opcua.DataType.Float,
                    value: parseFloat (energy.current)
                }));
                await session.writeSingleNode ('ns=1;s=/
                SmartPower/SmartPlug1/Energy/voltage', new
                opcua.Variant ({
                    dataType: opcua.DataType.Float,
                    value: parseFloat (energy.voltage)
                }));
                await session.writeSingleNode ('ns=1;s=/
                SmartPower/SmartPlug1/Energy/power', new
                opcua.Variant ({
                    dataType: opcua.DataType.Float,
                    value: parseFloat (energy.power)
                }));
            }
            else
            {
                let nodes = [
                    {
                    nodeId: 'ns=1;s=/SmartPower/SmartPlug1/
                    Energy/voltage',
```

```
                    attributeId: opcua.AttributeIds.Value,
                    value: {
                        statusCode: opcua.StatusCodes.Bad
                    },
                    },
                    {
                    nodeId: 'ns=1;s=/SmartPower/SmartPlug1/
                    Energy/current',
                    attributeId: opcua.AttributeIds.Value,
                    value: {
                        statusCode: opcua.StatusCodes.Bad
                    },
                    },
                    {
                    nodeId: 'ns=1;s=/SmartPower/SmartPlug1/
                    Energy/power',
                    attributeId: opcua.AttributeIds.Value,
                    value: {
                        statusCode: opcua.StatusCodes.Bad
                    },
                    }
                ];
                await session.write (nodes);
            }
        }
        catch (e)
        {
            console.error ('OPC UA server write error '+e.
            message);
        }
    }, 500);
```

In case of an error, we do not want to write an actual value to the server, but report a *Bad status* code. The `writeSingleNode()` function does not allow this, so we need to use the `write()` function. This receives a single parameter that is a list of nodes and values to be written. This is why we declare an array of objects, each object having the following properties:

- nodeId – The ID of the variable

- attributeId – The attribute of the node that we want to write to (in this case it is the value, others might have been the data type or the browseName)

- value – The value with properties that we want to write

In our case, for the value property, we only specify the `statusCode`.

Tip   We can make an optimization and write all the nodes at once when there is no error, just like we did in the case of an error. For this, the code should be modified as in Listing 6-13.

Listing 6-13. Optimized code

```
let nodes = [
    {
        nodeId: 'ns=1;s=/SmartPower/SmartPlug1/Energy/voltage',
        attributeId: opcua.AttributeIds.Value,
        value: {
            value: new opcua.Variant ({
                dataType: opcua.DataType.Float,
                value: parseFloat (energy.voltage)
            }),
          sourceTimestamp: new Date ()
        },
    },
```

```
    {
        nodeId: 'ns=1;s=/SmartPower/SmartPlug1/Energy/current',
        attributeId: opcua.AttributeIds.Value,
        value: {
            value: new opcua.Variant ({
                dataType: opcua.DataType.Float,
                value: parseFloat (energy.current)
            }),
sourceTimestamp: new Date ()
        },
    },
    {

        nodeId: 'ns=1;s=/SmartPower/SmartPlug1/Energy/power',
        attributeId: opcua.AttributeIds.Value,
        value: {
            value: new opcua.Variant ({
                dataType: opcua.DataType.Float,
                value: parseFloat (energy.power)
            }),
         sourceTimestamp: new Date ()
        },
    }
];
await session.write (nodes);
```

Caution   When writing variables, please make sure to add the
sourceTimestamp parameter and set it to the current date. This
marks the time when the variable was changed by the client. If this is
not present, the server sets it to null, and some clients are not able
to display the data.

Switch the Power Plug On and Off

Now let us implement the actual power switching functionality. We have a variable called SmartPower/PowerPlug1/power in the OPC UA Server. This is written by another component (most probably the UI) when it desires to switch the power plug on or off. Thus, we need to monitor the variable's changes and send the commands to the power plug. To do this, we have to create a subscription to the server. We need to add the code in Listing 6-14 after creating the session.

Listing 6-14. Subscribe to OPC UA Server

```
const subscription= opcua.ClientSubscription.create(session,{
    requestedPublishingInterval: 1000,
    requestedLifetimeCount: 10,
    requestedMaxKeepAliveCount: 2,
    maxNotificationsPerPublish: 10,
    publishingEnabled: true,
    priority: 10
});

subscription.on("started", ()=>{
    console.log ('SmartPlug subscribed to server');
});
```

The opcua.ClientSubscription.create() asks the OPC UA Server for a new subscription with the provided parameters. The function requires the parameters listed in Table 6-4.

Table 6-4. OPC UA client subscription parameters

Parameter	Description
requestedPublishingInterval	The interval, in milliseconds, at which the server should publish notifications to the client. Each client can have several subscriptions with different intervals. A publish messages can contain several notifications. A value of 0 means the server uses the smallest value that it can use. For example, a variable change is a notification.
requestedLifetimeCount	The subscription expires and is deleted by the server when there is no notification to be sent to the client this amount of times. The value has to be at least three times the *keepAliveCount*.
requestedMaxKeepaliveCount	If there is no notification to be sent this amount of times, the server sends a keep-alive notification.
maxNotificationsPerPublish	The number of notifications to send per each publish message, 0 is unlimited.
publishingEnabled	Enable or disable the publishing of notifications.
priority	The priority of the subscription, a higher number is a higher priority. Usually this should be left 0.

The subscription is created only when the started event is emitted. We are able to use the subscription variable before the event is emitted, but we get data only after the emitted event. After the subscription is in place, we can start monitoring variables. We need to monitor the SmartPower/PowerPlug1/power variable, so we use the code in Listing 6-15.

Listing 6-15. Monitor OPC UA variables

```
const smartPlug1 = await subscription.monitor({nodeId:'ns=1;
s=/SmartPower/SmartPlug1/power'},
    {
        samplingInterval: 500,
        discardOldest: true,
        queueSize: 1
    },
    opcua.TimestampsToReturn.Both);

smartPlug1.on ('changed', (data) => {
    // console.log (data.value.value);
    if (data.statusCode === opcua.StatusCodes.Good) {
        if (data.value.value === true)
        {
            smart.on (DEVICE_IP);
        }
        else
        {
            smart.off (DEVICE_IP)
        }
    }
});
```

The monitor function takes several parameters; each of them is described in Table 6-5.

Table 6-5. *OPC UA monitor variable parameters*

Parameter	Description
samplingInterval	This represents the period in milliseconds at which the server reads and checks if the variable has changed. A change means either the value, the timestamp, or the statusCode.
discardOldest	Every time a variable changes, it is added to a queue to be sent. If the queue is filled before it is sent, some values need to be discarded. Based on this parameter, the server discards the oldest or the newest value.
queueSize	The size of queue to store the values.

In our example, we instruct the server to read the value every 500ms. We are interested in the latest value, so we set a queue size of one and ask the server to discard the oldest value. This was, the server always sends us a single value, the latest one.

The server does not sample the value and report the changes to our client. The client emits the changed event. To take action when a value changes, we need to register a function for the changed event. The function takes as a parameter the data sent by the server. The properties of the data are shown in Table 6-6.

Table 6-6. *OPC UA value properties*

Property	Description
value	The Variant object that represents the value of the variable (dataType, value, etc.).
value.value	The value.
value.dataType	The OPC UA data type of the variable.
statusCode	The OPC UA status code (should be opcua.StatusCodes.Good if the value is the right one).
sourceTimestamp	The timestamp of the client that changed the value (can be null).
serverTimestamp	The timestamp of the server when it received the change from the client.

All we need to do when the value changes is to check if the status code is *Good* and send a command to the power plug depending on the value of the variable.

Putting It All Together

Now that we have all the components, let us connect them. In the **main. js** file, we need to import the *server* and the *driver*. The code should be the one in Listing 6-16.

Listing 6-16. Import the server and the driver

```
// start the OPC/UA server
require ('./server');

// start the power plug driver
require ('./driver');
```

All that is left now is to start the application. The user interface is the *ProSys OPC UA Client Application*. Please start it and connect to the OPC UA Server from the application. Browse to *PowerPlug1* and select the *Energy* folder. Right-click each of the *voltage, current,* and *power* variables and select *Monitor*. You should see them in *Data View* on the right-side panel. Next to each variable in the *Data View,* check the *Graph* box. Figure 6-11 shows how the display looks like.

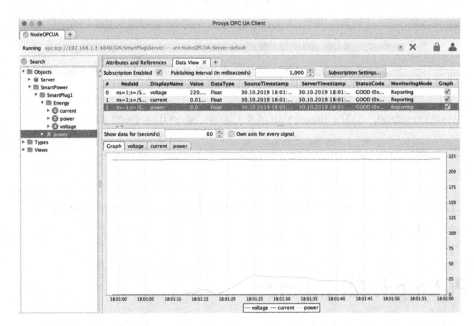

Figure 6-11. *OPC UA smart power GUI*

To turn the power plug on and off, right-click the *power* variable from the *SmartPlug1* folder and use *Write Value.* Select *true/false* to switch.

Summary

In this chapter, we have implemented a power consumption control system using industrial standards.

We first configured the TP-Link HS110 Smart Wi-Fi Plug to be controlled from a simple Python script, and we created an API for turning it on and off and retrieving consumption parameters. Further on, we created an OPC UA Server that stores values such as energy consumption or current voltage.

Finally, we used various OPC UA clients to monitor the data coming from the power plug and also to control it (turn the plug on/off).

The purpose of this example was to give an overview of how commercial and industrial systems are built in a modular way, making them easier to maintain and update.

CHAPTER 7

Data Storing and Processing

Many commercial and industrial IoT systems collect large amounts of data. It is currently expected that IoT devices will generate 80ZB (zettabytes, 1ZB = 1 billion terabytes) over the next decade. In most situations, due to the high volume and potential complex computational pipeline, real-time analysis of this data is very difficult, or impossible. As such, efficient and large-scale data storage capabilities are an essential component in IoT systems: we store the data and use edge or cloud hardware to process it over minutes, hours, or even days.

The applications we have built so far are designed to monitor the environment and take actions according to specific parameters. We also integrated web services so we can process the data we retrieve from the environment. However, we did not deal with actual storing of the information coming from the sensors. Any industrial system has a component that deals with data storage. As we need to keep large amounts of data, this is an essential aspect of any IoT application.

In this chapter, we will discuss about how to monitor and process data read from the smart power plugs. By using the project built in the previous chapter, we aim to extend it so we can connect several power plugs and store energy consumption information using MariaDB.[1]

---

[1] https://mariadb.org

© Ioana Culic; Alexandru Radovici; Cristian Rusu 2020
I. Culic et al., *Commercial and Industrial Internet of Things Applications with the Raspberry Pi*,
https://doi.org/10.1007/978-1-4842-5296-3_7

Necessary Components

As this chapter aims to build a prototype of an industrial project, we power the Raspberry Pi using power over Ethernet (PoE). This requires either a network switch that is PoE enabled or a PoE injector.

The PoE HAT is a small add-on for the Raspberry Pi 3+ or 4 that is able to connect a PoE-enabled network switch to the Raspberry Pi. This means that instead of using a power adapter, we can power the Raspberry Pi directly from the network cable. The second advantage of using the PoE HAT is that it has a fan that is cooling down the Raspberry SoC. To connect the HAT to the Raspberry Pi, you just need to place it on top of the board (Figure 7-1). You can also solder a pin line to the HAT, so it exposes the Raspberry Pi's pins.

Figure 7-1. *Raspberry Pi PoE HAT*[2]

The Raspberry Pi's *hard drive* is an SD card. While these cards are fine for prototyping, working with them in industrial environments is not recommended as they tend to break after some time. While fixing

---

[2]https://grobotronics.com/raspberry-pi-power-over-ethernet-poe-hat.html?sl=en

a broken SD card is usually just a matter of writing the Raspberry Pi SD card image and, if needed, swapping it with a new one, recovering stored data is an issue. In this chapter, we collect a fair amount of data on energy consumption, data that we do not want to lose. This is why we recommend using an external storage system to store the actual data.

For this chapter, we will need

- One Raspberry Pi connected to Wyliodrin STUDIO.

- One or more TP-Link HS110 Smart Power Plug.

- One Raspberry Pi PoE HAT (optional, requires a Raspberry Pi 3+ or 4).

- A PoE (802.3af) capable network switch or PoE injector (optional).

- External hard drive or SSD drive (optional, a USB 3.0 device is recommended).

Note   You may use any other smart power plug. The only requirement is that it should have some open API that you can use to control it. Some of the smart power plugs only work with their specific phone apps and cloud systems.

Use MariaDB to Store Data

While storing small amounts of information may be done using files, when storing large amounts of data, a database system is required. There are a lot of database systems that you can use to store data; some are summarized in Table 7-1.

Table 7-1. *Database systems*

Name	Storage Type	Description
MariaDB	Relational	Developed by MariaDB Foundation; it is a fully open source database system licensed under GPL v2. It is a fork of MySQL developed by the original MySQL developers.
MySQL	Relational	Developed by Oracle; it is a partially open source database system, having a community edition (free) and professional (paid) editions.
PostgreSQL	Relational	Developed by PostgreSQL Global Development Group; it is a fully open source database system licensed under a proprietary license (compatible with GPL). The project started at UC Berkeley in 1986.
SQLite	Relational	A file storage open source database developed by the SQLite Consortium licensed under LGPL. This is an embeddable database system.
MongoDB	NoSQL, Document	A partially open source document database system built by MongoDB. It is licensed under a proprietary license.
Redis	Key/Value, List, In Memory	An open source in memory database, licensed under BSD-3 license, sponsored by Redis Labs, VMWare, and Pivotal. Data storage is in memory and may be stored on a drive. It is usually used for cached data storage.

Install MariaDB

We have chosen MariaDB to store the data coming from the smart power monitoring systems as it is fully open source, is compatible with MySQL (one of the most popular database systems), has a simple architecture, and has a large community for support and examples.

Now let us install MariaDB on the Raspberry Pi. Using Wyliodrin STUDIO, connect to the Raspberry Pi and open a *SHELL tab*. There is a MariaDB package in the Raspbian repository, so we run apt to update the packages database and then install MariaDB (Listing 7-1).

Listing 7-1. Install MariaDB

```
sudo apt-get update
sudo apt-get install mariadb-server
```

To check if MariaDB is properly installed, we run the MariaDB monitor: sudo mariadb. If there is no error, the MariaDB monitor should display a text similar to Listing 7-2.

Listing 7-2. MariaDB install check

```
Welcome to the MariaDB monitor. Commands end with ; or \g.
Your MariaDB connection id is 1440
Server version: 10.3.17-MariaDB-0+deb10u1 Raspbian 10

Copyright (c) 2000, 2018, Oracle, MariaDB Corporation Ab and
others.

Type 'help;' or '\h' for help. Type '\c' to clear the current
input statement.

MariaDB [(none)]>
```

Use the exit command to exit the MariaDB monitor.

Note   The version displayed by your monitor might be different.

External Storage Setup

The Raspberry Pi's primary data storage is the SD card. SD cards are easy to use but are not fail-safe, so storing large amounts of data on them is not recommended.

Note   The following step is optional. The system works without it, but be aware that you can lose the stored data at any time. If you do not want to install any external hard drive or SSD, skip to the next section.

For the data storage, we need an external USB Hard Drive or SSD. We recommend a USB 3 device as it is faster. Plug in the USB storage device and wait for a few seconds, then run the dmesg command in the shell. It should display something similar to Listing 7-3.

Tip   We recommend using an external SSD instead of a hard drive as the SSD consumes less power. The Raspberry Pi may not be able to supply the necessary power for a hard drive.

Listing 7-3. Attaching a hard drive or SSD over USB

```
pi@raspberrypi:~$ dmesg
[162930.926074] usb 1-1.1: new high-speed USB device number 3
using xhci_hcd
[162931.056976] usb 1-1.1: New USB device found, idVendor=04e8,
idProduct=6032, bcdDevice= 0.00
```

```
[162931.056992] usb 1-1.1: New USB device strings: Mfr=1,
Product=11, SerialNumber=3
[162931.057005] usb 1-1.1: Product: Samsung G2 Portable
[162931.057017] usb 1-1.1: Manufacturer: JMicron
[162931.057028] usb 1-1.1: SerialNumber: 00000011E0A2A
[162931.059388] usb-storage 1-1.1:1.0: USB Mass Storage device
detected
[162931.059859] scsi host0: usb-storage 1-1.1:1.0
[162932.131493] scsi 0:0:0:0: Direct-Access     Samsung  G2
Portable          PQ: 0 ANSI: 2 CCS
[162932.132442] sd 0:0:0:0: [sda] 625142448 512-byte logical
blocks: (320 GB/298 GiB)
[162932.133128] sd 0:0:0:0: [sda] Write Protect is off
[162932.133143] sd 0:0:0:0: [sda] Mode Sense: 3c 00 00 00
[162932.133823] sd 0:0:0:0: [sda] Write cache: disabled, read
cache: enabled, doesn't support DPO or FUA
[162932.151210] sd 0:0:0:0: Attached scsi generic sg0 type 0
[162932.165427] sda: sda1
[162932.168533] sd 0:0:0:0: [sda] Attached SCSI disk
```

Using dmesg, we can find out the device file name that has been mapped to the hard drive. It should look similar to sdX: sdX1 sdX2... where sdX is the name of the drive and sdX1...sdXn are the names of the partitions of the drive. In our example, you can see we have the drive name sda and that it has only one partition: sda1.

Note   If you do not see a line similar to the one in Listing 7-3, there might not be a partition table on the drive. To create a partition table, run fdisk and create a DOS partition table. Listing 7-4 shows an example for a new drive.

Listing 7-4. Create a new partition table

```
pi@raspberrypi:~$ sudo fdisk /dev/sda

Welcome to fdisk (util-linux 2.33.1).
Changes will remain in memory only, until you decide to write
them.
Be careful before using the write command.

Command (m for help): o
Created a new DOS disklabel with disk identifier 0xa756425e.

Command (m for help): w
The partition table has been altered.
Syncing disks.
```

Tip   The letters in bold are the commands that we introduced.

Now let us start setting up the disk drive. First, we run fdisk and create the partition (Listing 7-5).

Caution   We assume the whole disk drive is used for storing data and thus erase all its contents. If you have any other data stored on the drive, either back it up or set up the disk in a different manner.

Listing 7-5. Create new partition

```
pi@raspberrypi:~ $ sudo fdisk /dev/sda

Welcome to fdisk (util-linux 2.33.1).
Changes will remain in memory only, until you decide to write them.
Be careful before using the write command.
```

Command (m for help): **p**
Disk /dev/sda: 223.6 GiB, 240057409536 bytes, 468862128 sectors
Disk model: KINGSTON SUV5002
Units: sectors of 1 * 512 = 512 bytes
Sector size (logical/physical): 512 bytes / 512 bytes
I/O size (minimum/optimal): 512 bytes / 512 bytes
Disklabel type: dos
Disk identifier: 0xa756425e

Command (m for help): **n**
Partition type
    p   primary (0 primary, 0 extended, 4 free)
    e   extended (container for logical partitions)
Select (default p): **p**
Partition number (1-4, default 1): **1**
First sector (2048-468862127, default 2048):
Last sector, +/-sectors or +/-size{K,M,G,T,P} (2048-468862127,
default 468862127):
Created a new partition 1 of type 'Linux' and of size 223.6 GiB.

Command (m for help): **p**
Disk /dev/sda: 223.6 GiB, 240057409536 bytes, 468862128 sectors
Disk model: KINGSTON SUV5002
Units: sectors of 1 * 512 = 512 bytes
Sector size (logical/physical): 512 bytes / 512 bytes
I/O size (minimum/optimal): 512 bytes / 512 bytes
Disklabel type: dos
Disk identifier: 0xa756425e

Device   Boot Start   End   Sectors   Size Id Type
/dev/sda1 2048 468862127 468860080 223.6G 83 Linux

Command (m for help): **w**

The partition table has been altered.
Calling ioctl() to re-read partition table.
Syncing disks.

Note   Values for your drive might be different.

We have used the p command to print the partition table. There are no partitions on our drive. Next, we need to create a Linux partition for the whole drive. The command for a new partition is n.

Now we should have one Linux partition for the whole drive. Creating the partition is not enough; before we can use it, we have to format it so we can set up a file system. This is done by running the mkfs.ext4 command, like shown in Listing 7-6.

Listing 7-6. Formatting the external storage drive

```
pi@raspberrypi:~ $ sudo mkfs.ext4 /dev/sda1
mke2fs 1.44.5 (15-Dec-2018)
Creating filesystem with 58607510 4k blocks and 14655488 inodes
Filesystem UUID: 6266a2d7-dbbc-441a-9d6d-014e1b7db54d
Superblock backups stored on blocks:
        32768, 98304, 163840, 229376, 294912, 819200, 884736,
        1605632, 2654208,n4096000, 7962624, 11239424, 20480000,
        23887872

Allocating group tables: done
Writing inode tables: done
Creating journal (262144 blocks): done
Writing superblocks and filesystem accounting information: done
```

Now that we have the drive connected and the partition is formatted, we have to mount it (Listing 7-7). Mounting is the action of displaying the partition contents in the file system. The command that we use to achieve this is mount. First, we have to create an empty folder that is the mount point. Its content is replaced by the actual drive partition contents. Usually these folders are in the **/mnt** directory.

Listing 7-7. Mount the external drive storage

```
pi@raspberrypi:~ $ sudo mkdir /mnt/storage
pi@raspberrypi:~ $ sudo mount /dev/sda1 /mnt/storage
pi@raspberrypi:~ $ ls -l /mnt/storage
total 16
drwx------ 2 root root 16384 Nov  4 15:45 lost+found
```

The first command in Listing 7-7 creates the folder where the external drive is mounted. The second command actually mounts the drive (/dev/sda1) to the folder (/mnt/storage). The third command displays the contents of the mounted drive.

Note   All Linux partitions have a folder called **lost+found**; this is why the newly created partition is not empty.

Once we mounted the device, it remains in this state until we manually run umount, restart, or shut down the Raspberry Pi.

To make sure the drive gets mounted every time the Raspberry Pi starts, and we do not have to repeat the previous commands, we can specify this in the **/etc/fstab** file. This file describes the drives that need to be mounted at startup. To achieve this, we have to add an extra line similar to the one shown in Listing 7-8. To edit the file, we use nano and run the following command in the SHELL tab: sudo nano /etc/fstab.

Listing 7-8. Add the external storage in **/etc/fstab**

```
proc        /proc    proc  defaults        0      0
PARTUUID=3778ffa5-01 /boot vfat defaults  0   2
PARTUUID=3778ffa5-02 /        ext4 defaults,noatime 0 1
# a swapfile is not a swap partition, no line here
# use  dphys-swapfile swap[on|off]  for that
```
/dev/sda1 /mnt/storage auto defaults 0 0

Note   Press *Ctrl+X* to exit the nano editor. Make sure you save the file when asked.

The emphasized line in Listing 7-8 is the line we added. This instructs the Raspberry Pi's operating system to mount **/dev/sda1** in **/mnt/storage** while auto-detecting the file system from the partition (**auto**) and using the default mount flags.

Now, let us reboot the Raspberry Pi to verify if this works. When the Raspberry Pi restarts, run the mount command in the SHELL tab to list all the mounted drives. If **/dev/sda1** appears in the list, the device was successfully mounted (Listing 7-9).

Listing 7-9. All the Raspberry Pi mounted drives

```
pi@raspberrypi:~ $ mount
/dev/mmcblk0p2 on / type ext4 (rw,noatime)
devtmpfs on /dev type devtmpfs (rw,relatime,size=860916k,
nr_inodes=122234,mode=755)
sysfs on /sys type sysfs (rw,nosuid,nodev,noexec,relatime)
proc on /proc type proc (rw,relatime)
... (parts of the listing have been deleted as they are not
relevant)
```
/dev/sda1 on /mnt/storage type ext4 (rw,relatime)

```
/dev/mmcblk0p1 on /boot type vfat (rw,relatime,fmask=0022,
dmask=0022,codepage=437,iocharset=ascii,shortname=mixed,errors=
remount-ro)
overlay on
```

Now that we have an external storage system mounted, we have to configure MariaDB to store the databases on the storage system. First, inside **/mnt/storage**, we create a folder called **smartpower**. Inside **smartpower**, we create a new folder, called **database**. Listing 7-10 shows the commands used and the expected result.

Listing 7-10. Create the external storage folder layout

```
pi@raspberrypi:~ $ sudo mkdir /mnt/storage/smartpower
pi@raspberrypi:~ $ sudo mkdir /mnt/storage/smartpower/database
pi@raspberrypi:~ $ tree /mnt/storage
/mnt/storage
├── lost+found [error opening dir]
└── smartpower
    └── database

3 directories, 0 files
```

Tip   The tree command displays the contents of a folder in a tree structure. It is not installed by default and can be installed using sudo apt-get install tree. You can also visualize the tree structure by using the *File Manager* option in Wyliodrin STUDIO.

We store the database information inside the **/mnt/storage/ smartpower/database** folder. For this, we need to initialize the folder with an empty database. MariaDB supports a command that creates an empty database inside a folder (mysql_install_db). Listing 7-11 shows the command we run.

Listing 7-11. Create an empty MariaDB database

```
pi@raspberrypi:~ $ sudo mysql_install_db --user=mysql
--datadir=/mnt/storage/smartpower/database
Installing MariaDB/MySQL system tables in '/mnt/storage/
smartpower/database' ...
OK
```

... (*some of the listing has been deleted as it had no relevant
information*)

The next step is to configure MariaDB to use the newly created
database folder. MariaDB's settings are specified in the **/etc/mysql/
mariadb.conf.d/50-server.cnf** file. Here we mention the directory where
the information needs to be stored. Again, we use nano to edit the file
(Listing 7-12).

Listing 7-12. MariaDB settings file with the new database directory
(in bold)

```
pi@raspberrypi:~ $ sudo nano /etc/mysql/mariadb.conf.d/50-
server.cnf

#
# These groups are read by MariaDB server.
# Use it for options that only the server (but not #clients)
should see
#
# See the examples of server my.cnf files in #/usr/share/mysql

# this is read by the standalone daemon and embedded #servers
[server]

# this is only for the mysqld standalone daemon
[mysqld]
```

```
#
# * Basic Settings
#
user              = mysql
pid-file          = /run/mysqld/mysqld.pid
socket            = /run/mysqld/mysqld.sock
#port             = 3306
basedir           = /usr
#datadir          = /var/lib/mysql
datadir           = /mnt//storage/smartpower/database
tmpdir            = /tmp
lc-messages-dir   = /usr/share/mysql
#skip-external-locking

# Instead of skip-networking the default is now to #listen only
on localhost which is more compatible #and is not less secure.
bind-address      = 127.0.0.1
```

Now let us restart MariaDB so that it uses the new database path. Run the sudo service mariadb restart command in the SHELL tab. If there is no error, everything should be working fine.

You can run sudo mariadb to verify that the new settings work. If this command is successful and it shows you a MariaDB database prompt, the new settings have been successfully implemented.

Set Up the Data Model

We use MariaDB to store power consumption data from several smart power plugs. Every five seconds, we store the instantaneous voltage, current, and power. In addition, we store the relay state, which tells us whether the power plug is on or off.

Now that we are aware of the data that we need to store, we can establish how this can be structured. MariaDB is a relational database, meaning that the data is stored in tables. A row in a table represents one item. For our example, we have one table for the metrics we collect and one table for the relay status.

The first item we need to create is the database, which we call smartpower. For this, we first start the MariaDB monitor using the sudo mariadb command. Next, we can type commands that allow us to store and retrieve data. To create a new database, we need to use the CREATE DATABASE command. To use the database, we need to open it first using the USE command. After opening a database, MariaDB monitor shows its name in the prompt (Listing 7-13).

Note   In the MariaDB system, a database is a collection of tables. Think of a database as a folder and of tables as files.

Listing 7-13. Create the MariaDB **smartpower** database

```
MariaDB [(none)]> CREATE DATABASE smartpower;
Query OK, 1 row affected (0.001 sec)
MariaDB [(none)]> USE smartpower;
Database changed
MariaDB [smartpower]>
```

We create the metrics table using the CREATE TABLE command. Listing 7-14 shows the exact command. Our table has six columns presented in Table 7-2.

Listing 7-14. Create the metrics table

```
MariaDB [smartpower]> CREATE TABLE meters (id INT AUTO_INCREMENT
PRIMARY KEY NOT NULL, timestamp TIMESTAMP NOT NULL, smartplug
VARCHAR(200) NOT NULL, voltage FLOAT, current FLOAT, power FLOAT);
Query OK, 0 rows affected (0.012 sec)
```

Table 7-2. *The MariaDB table structure*

Name	Data Type	Description
id	INT	An ID for each table entry; this is the primary key. Its purpose is to uniquely identify a table entry or row.
timestamp	TIMESTAMP	The date and time when the entry or row was inserted in the table. The TIMESTAMP data type will instruct MariaDB to automatically fill this field with the current timestamp when the entry or row is inserted.
smartplug	VARCHAR (200)	The name of the smart plug to which the newly inserted values belong to. We use the same table for storing the values from all the smart plugs. That is why one of the fields identifies the smart plug.
voltage	FLOAT	The voltage value.
current	FLOAT	The current value.
power	FLOAT	The power value.

In Listing 7-14, we can notice that we have used some flags next to the data types. Let us go through each of them to understand their purpose better. The AUTO_INCREMENT flag for the id field makes MariaDB add a new unique value to the id field each time a row is inserted. The first time we insert a row, the value inserted in the id field is 1. The next time we insert a row, the value is 2. The PRIMARY KEY flag marks the field as an index, so searching for a specific row using this field is fast. Each table needs one and only one primary key. The NOT NULL flags prevent MariaDB to insert a row into the table if that field value is NULL.

Note   Relational databases can differentiate between a field that stores a value and a field that has a value missing. For example, in our case, we have a field that stores the power consumption value. If for some reason, the smart plug goes offline and we cannot read it, it does not mean the value does not exist, we just do not know it. If we were to write 0 into the field, that would be wrong as the power was not 0W. We can write a NULL value (different from 0), and that marks that we do not know the value.

To make sure the table was created according to the specified settings, we can run the DESCRIBE command, which prints all table fields and their properties (Figure 7-2).

```
MariaDB [smartpower]> DESCRIBE meters;
+-----------+--------------+------+-----+-------------------+-----------------------------+
| Field     | Type         | Null | Key | Default           | Extra                       |
+-----------+--------------+------+-----+-------------------+-----------------------------+
| id        | int(11)      | NO   | PRI | NULL              | auto_increment              |
| timestamp | timestamp    | NO   |     | current_timestamp()| on update current_timestamp()|
| smartplug | varchar(200) | NO   | MUL | NULL              |                             |
| voltage   | float        | YES  |     | NULL              |                             |
| current   | float        | YES  |     | NULL              |                             |
| power     | float        | YES  |     | NULL              |                             |
+-----------+--------------+------+-----+-------------------+-----------------------------+
6 rows in set (0.003 sec)
```

Figure 7-2. *Display meters table properties*

There is one more step that we have to take before having the table in place. We have a field called smartplug that is of type string and which stores the name of the smart plug to which the data in that row belongs to. When we query this table, we ask MariaDB to show us all the values for one of the smart plugs. The SQL query looks like the one in Listing 7-15. The query is not very fast as MariaDB has to search all the table rows and match the value of smartplug. To make it faster, we have to define an index for the smartplug field, by using the CREATE INDEX command illustrated in Figure 7-3.

Listing 7-15. Querying the meter values for the smart plug **SmartPlug1**

```
SELECT * FROM meters WHERE smartplug = 'SmartPlug1';
```

```
MariaDB [smartpower]> CREATE INDEX meterssmartplug ON meters (smartplug);
Query OK, 0 rows affected (0.053 sec)
Records: 0  Duplicates: 0  Warnings: 0

MariaDB [smartpower]> SHOW INDEXES IN meters;
+--------+------------+-----------------+--------------+-------------+-----------+-------------+----------+--------+------+------------+---------+---------------+
| Table  | Non_unique | Key_name        | Seq_in_index | Column_name | Collation | Cardinality | Sub_part | Packed | Null | Index_type | Comment | Index_comment |
+--------+------------+-----------------+--------------+-------------+-----------+-------------+----------+--------+------+------------+---------+---------------+
| meters |          0 | PRIMARY         |            1 | id          | A         |       10528 | NULL     | NULL   |      | BTREE      |         |               |
| meters |          1 | meterssmartplug |            1 | smartplug   | A         |           4 | NULL     | NULL   |      | BTREE      |         |               |
+--------+------------+-----------------+--------------+-------------+-----------+-------------+----------+--------+------+------------+---------+---------------+
2 rows in set (0.001 sec)
```

Figure 7-3. *Create an index for the **smartplug** field*

Defining an index makes searching the table fast every time we have this field in the WHERE clause.

Tip   When using MariaDB and searching in tables, make sure you have indexes for every item in the WHERE clause.

Now, let us create a table to store the status of the smart plug. Similarly to the meters table, we use the CREATE TABLE command. This table is called onoff, and it has one entry for each smartplug, making the smartplug field a PRIMARY KEY (Listing 7-16).

Listing 7-16. Create the onoff table to store the smart plug status

```
MariaDB [smartpower]> CREATE TABLE onoff (timestamp TIMESTAMP,
smartplug VARCHAR (200) PRIMARY KEY, relay INT NOT NULL);
Query OK, 0 rows affected (0.018 sec)
```

Having created these two tables, our database is complete. To be able to access the database from a piece of software, we have to create a user and a password, but we will discuss these things later.

Upgrade to Use Multiple Smart Plugs

To build the project in this chapter, we start from the project built in the previous chapter and make some modifications to it. We interface several smart plugs (instead of one), modify the OPC UA model, and access the MariaDB database and store the data.

We extend the architecture of the previous project by adding a database module. This module queries the OPC UA Server at a fixed time interval and stores the data, voltage, current, power, and relay in the MariaDB database. Figure 7-4 presents the new architecture.

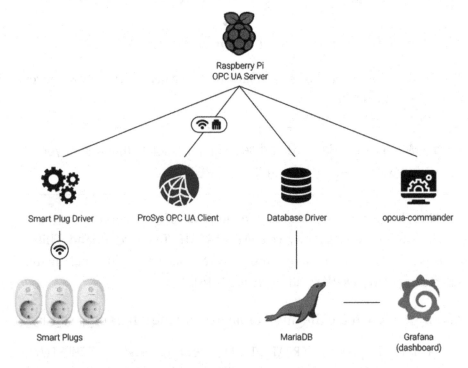

Figure 7-4. *The software architecture*

Another modification is to introduce a list of smart plugs. In the main folder of the project, we need to add a file called **plugs.json**. This contains a list of smart plugs that we want to monitor. For this example, we monitor two smart plugs, as can be seen in Listing 7-17.

Listing 7-17. Smart plugs list in **plugs.json**

```
[
    {
        "name": "SmartPlug1",
        "ip": "192.168.1.72"
    },
    {
        "name": "SmartPlug2",
        "ip": "192.168.1.169"
    }
]
```

Caution   You need to set up both smart plugs before you can use them. You can follow the steps described in **Chapter** 6 to set up IP addresses for both power plugs.

The OPC UA Data Model

For the OPC UA data model, we use a similar model to the one in the previous chapter. We need to make the following changes:

1. We defined for each smart plug a folder called **Energy** that stores the power (voltage, current, and power) variables.

2. For each smart plug, we defined a folder called
    Actions that stores the variable **switch**. This is a
    Boolean variable that is used as a function. This
    variable is monitored by the smart plug driver, and
    every time it changes, the driver switches the smart
    plug on or off, according to the variable's new value.

3. Each smart plug has a folder called **Sysinfo**, where
    we declare two variables: a String called alias and
    a Boolean called relay.

The initial data model, designed using visual blocks, is shown in
Figure 7-5. The model is good, but it is not enough. This project has to be
able to get data from several smart plugs, each smart plug having the same
data model. The only difference between the plugs is the way the data
model is called. You can see from the way the model looks that right now it
is designed to serve only one smart plug, SmartPlug1.

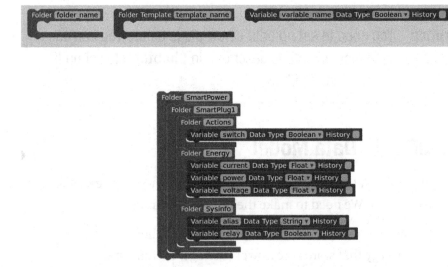

Figure 7-5. *OPC UA smart plug data model*

A feature that Wyliodrin STUDIO OPC UA Visual model editor provides is *templates*. This works similar to an OPC UA Folder; it contains other subfolders and variables. The difference is that when the server runs, it creates a new folder for each smart plug based on the template. Figure 7-6 shows the data model created using the template.

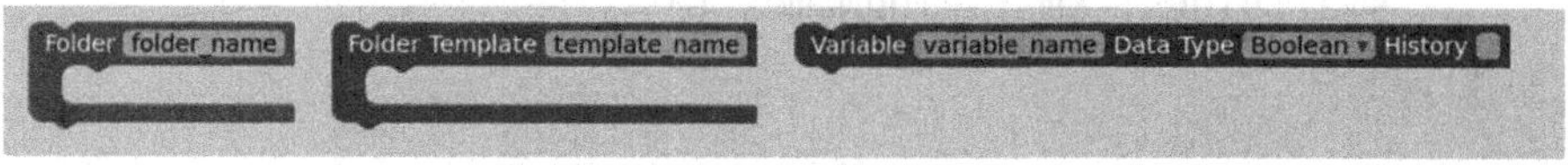

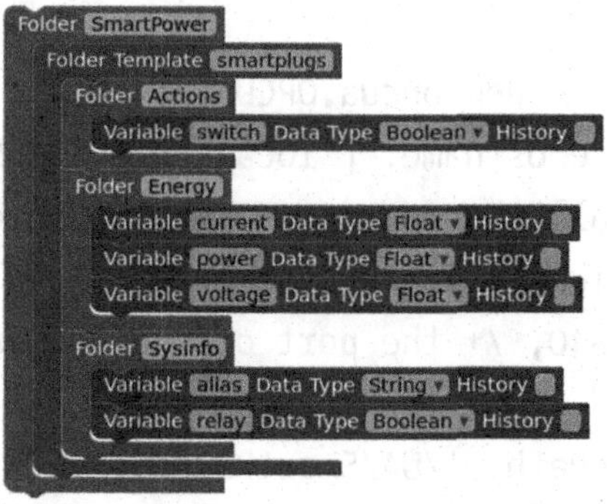

Figure 7-6. *OPC UA data model using a template*

Now, let us load the data model into the server. The server source code is the same as for the project described in the previous chapter, with a small change when it comes to loading the data model (Listing 7-18).

Listing 7-18. The OPC UA Server

```
const opcua = require('node-opcua');
const plugs = require ('../plugs.json');

function smartPlugNames ()
{
    let smartplugs = [];
    for (let plug of plugs) smartplugs.push (plug.name);
```

```javascript
    return smartplugs;
}

function loadModel (server)
{
    require ('./settings.opcuamodel.js')(server, {
        smartplugs: smartPlugNames ()
    });
}

async function run ()
{
    const server = new opcua.OPCUAServer({
        alternateHostname: ['localhost', '192.168.1.3'],
        /* add all the addresses for the interfaces that you
        would like to listen to*/
        port: 4840, /* the port of the listening socket of the
        server*/
        resourcePath: '/UA/SmartPlugsServer', /* this path will
        be added to the endpoint resource name*/
        buildInfo : {
            productName: 'SmartPlugs Server',
            buildNumber: '1',
            buildDate: new Date()
        }
    });

    try
    {
        await server.start ();
        loadModel (server);
```

```
        console.log ('Server started at '+server.endpoints[0].
        endpointDescriptions()[0].endpointUrl);
    }
    catch (e)
    {
        console.error ('Server error: '+e.message);
    }
}
run ();
```

Let us run over the changes we made. First, we imported the plugs.
json file that contains the database of smart plugs. It actually contains an
array of objects defining each smart plug's name and IP address. The first
step is to store the database in the plugs variable by using the require
function.

The next change was made inside the loadModel() function. In the
previously described project, we imported the model giving it the OPC UA
server variable as a parameter. The new model uses templates, so we have
to add another parameter defining how the templates are used.
This parameter expects a JavaScript object that has a property (key) for
each of the models, each key identifying an array of folder names for which
the template is used. If you take a look at Figure 7-5, you can notice that
our template is called smartplugs. The object that we send as the second
parameter to the model has a property called smartplugs that takes the
value returned by the smartPlugNames() function. This function returns
an array of names for the smart plugs computed from the smart plugs
database (plugs.json).

Next, let us take a look at the smartPlugNames() function. It defines an
empty array and then iterates (using for-in) over the smart plugs database
(array of objects containing the name and IP of each smart plug), adding
into the array the name of each smart plug. After the iteration, it returns
the array containing the smart plug names.

If we start the server, we can see the two smart plugs using the ProSys OPC UA Client, just as illustrated in Figure 7-7. For each of the smart plugs in the database (plugs.json), we can see the template applied.

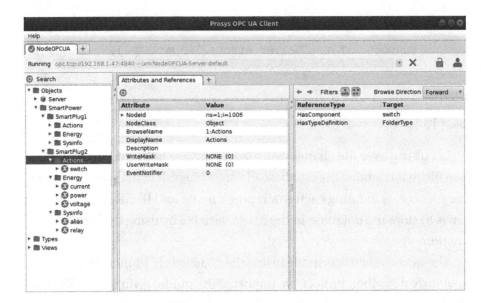

Figure 7-7. *ProSys OPC UA Client displaying the two smart plugs*

The New Smart Plug Driver

This component handles the connection between our software and the smart plugs. It is more or less the same driver like the one in the previous chapter, just that now it handles several smart plugs.

Note   All the files that we talk about in this section are stored in the driver folder of the project.

The first file that we have to modify is **tplink_smartplug.js**. Here, we add a function that reads the system information. To be able to use the function from outside the file, we also have to export it. This code is shown in Listing 7-19.

Listing 7-19. The readSysinfo() function added to **the tplink_ smartplug.js** file

```
async function readSysinfo (deviceIp)
{
    let sysinfo = {};
    let js = await tplinkSmartplug (deviceIp, 'info');
    if (js.system && js.system.get_sysinfo && js.system.get_
    sysinfo.err_code === 0)
    {
        sysinfo = js.system.get_sysinfo;
    }
    return sysinfo;
}
...
module.exports.readSysinfo = readSysinfo;
```

The body for the readSysinfo() function is very similar to the body for readEnergy(). The only difference is that we send the info instead of the energy command. There is also a small difference in how we check if there is an error (the object returned by the smart plug is different).

Next, we have to modify the **index.js** file. Here, we have made several changes to make the source code more generic and adapt it to support multiple smart plugs.

Writing values to the OPC UA Server has been done in the previous chapter using the functions provided by the OPC UA library. The source code is pretty big, and considering that here we have to repeat it for every smart plug that we control, we decided to define some new functions.

First, we define a function called writeValues() that allows us to write values to the OPC UA Server. This function is displayed in Listing 7-20. It receives two parameters: session, which is the OPC UA session, and values, which is an array of values to be written. Each item in the array has the following properties:

- nodeId – The ID of the variable to be written to.

- dataType – The OPC UA data type of the value to be written to the variable.

- value – The value to be written to the variable.

Listing 7-20. The writeValues() function that writes values to the OPC UA Server

```
function writeValues(session, values) {
    let nodes = [];
    for (let valueData of values) {
        nodes.push({
            nodeId: valueData.nodeId,
            attributeId: opcua.AttributeIds.Value,
            value: {
                value: new opcua.Variant({
                    dataType: valueData.dataType,
                    value: valueData.value,
                    statusCode: opcua.StatusCodes.Good,
                }),
                sourceTimestamp: new Date()
            },
        });
    }
    return session.write(nodes);
}
```

The writeValues() function iterates the list of values to be written and creates the actual list of nodes that are supplied to the OPC UA write() function. The write() function requires several properties for each variable it writes to, but most of the properties' values are the same for all our variables. All our variables have the status code set to Good, the sourceTimestamp set to the current timestamp, and the attributeId always set to opcua. AttributesIds.Value. This is why we set these static properties, and we do not need to pass these as parameters when calling writeValues().

The next function that we have to define is writeBadValues(). This takes as parameters the OPC UA session and a list of variable IDs and sets the status code of these variables to Bad. We use this function when a smart plug is not available. Listing 7-21 displays the source code.

Listing 7-21. The writeBadValues() function

```
function writeBadValues(session, nodeIds) {
    let nodes = [];
    for (let nodeId of nodeIds) {
        nodes.push({
            nodeId,
            attributeId: opcua.AttributeIds.Value,
            value: {
                statusCode: opcua.StatusCodes.Bad,
            },
            sourceTimestamp: new Date()
        });
    }
    return session.write(nodes);
}
```

This function does not write any actual value to the variables, it just sets the status code. We use this function when the smart plug that we try to read the values from is not available or is offline.

Now, let us get the information from the smart plugs. For this, we have defined a function called setupDevice(). This function receives as parameters the OPC UA session, the OPC UA subscription, and the smart plug information from the **plugs.json** file. The function's purpose is to start monitoring the switch variable so that it can turn the smart plug on and off, read the power values (voltage, current, and power) and system information (alias and relay status) from the smart plug, and write them to the OPC UA Server (Listing 7-22).

Listing 7-22. Getting data from the smart plug to the OPC UA Server

```
async function setupDevice(session, subscription, plug) {
    const smartPlug = await subscription.monitor({ nodeId:
    'ns=1;s=/SmartPower/' + plug.name + '/Actions/switch' },
        {
            samplingInterval: 500,
            discardOldest: true,
            queueSize: 1
        },
        opcua.TimestampsToReturn.Both);

    smartPlug.on('changed', (data) => {
        if (data.statusCode === opcua.StatusCodes.Good) {
            if (data.value.value === true) {
                smart.on(plug.ip);
            }
            else {
                smart.off(plug.ip)
            }
        }
    });
```

```
setInterval(async () => {
    try {
        let energy = await smart.readEnergy(plug.ip);
        if (energy.err_code === 0) {
            let values = [
                {
                    nodeId: 'ns=1;s=/SmartPower/' + plug.
                    name + '/Energy/voltage',
                    dataType: opcua.DataType.Float,
                    value: energy.voltage,
                },
                {
                    nodeId: 'ns=1;s=/SmartPower/' + plug.
                    name + '/Energy/current',
                    dataType: opcua.DataType.Float,
                    value: energy.current
                },
                {
                    nodeId: 'ns=1;s=/SmartPower/' + plug.
                    name + '/Energy/power',
                    dataType: opcua.DataType.Float,
                    value: energy.power
                }
            ];
            await writeValues(session, values);
        }
        else {
            let nodes = [
                'ns=1;s=/SmartPower/' + plug.name +
                '/Energy/voltage',
                'ns=1;s=/SmartPower/' + plug.name +
                '/Energy/current',
```

```
                'ns=1;s=/SmartPower/' + plug.name +
                '/Energy/power'
            ];
            await writeBadValues(session, nodes);
        }
    }
    catch (e) {
        console.error('OPC UA server energy write error ' +
        e.message);
    }
}, 3000);

setInterval(async () => {
    try {
        let sysinfo = await smart.readSysinfo(plug.ip);
        if (sysinfo.err_code === 0) {
            let values = [
                {
                    nodeId: 'ns=1;s=/SmartPower/' + plug.
                    name + '/Sysinfo/alias',
                    dataType: opcua.DataType.String,
                    value: sysinfo.alias,
                },
                {
                    nodeId: 'ns=1;s=/SmartPower/' + plug.
                    name + '/Sysinfo/relay',
                    dataType: opcua.DataType.Boolean,
                    value: (sysinfo.relay_state === 1) ?
                    true : false,
                }
            ];
```

```
        await writeValues(session, values);
    }
    else {
        let nodes = [
            'ns=1;s=/SmartPower/' + plug.name +
            '/Sysinfo/relay'
        ];
        await writeBadValues(session, nodes);
    }
}
catch (e) {
    console.error('OPC UA server relay write error ' +
    e.message);
}
}, 3000);
}
```

First, the function starts monitoring the switch variable. We set a
sampling rate of 500ms, as we want a small delay between the time the
user changes the value of the switch variable and the smart plug actually
switches the relay. We only need the newest value, so we can discard
the old values and set the queue size to 1. Every time the switch variable
changes, we send the corresponding command to the smart plug.

Note   Each smart plug is represented in the **plugs.json** file by an
object with two properties: name that is the name of the smart plug
and ip the IP address of the smart plug.

Next, we set a timer that reads the power values from the smart plug
every three seconds and writes them to the OPC UA Server. The code used
for writing the values to the OPC UA Server is more straightforward than

the one we wrote in the previous chapter. For each variable, we specified only three parameters: the ID, the data type, and the value. Then, we can call the writeValues() function that we defined previously. If there is an error while reading the power values, we call the writeBadValues() function with the list of the variables for the power values. This sets the variables' status code to Bad, and any user that reads them from the OPC UA Server knows that there was an error.

Using the same timer method, we add another timer that reads the system information from the smart plug every three seconds and writes the alias and relay_status variables to the OPC UA Server. In case of an error, we write only the status code Bad for the relay_state as the alias name has probably not changed when the smart plug is offline.

Next, we change the run() function that connects to the OPC UA Server. The connection code stays the same, we have to set up all the smart plugs. This is done using our previously defined function. Listing 7-23 illustrates the code. We iterate the plugs array and call the setupDevice() function for every smart plug.

Listing 7-23. The function that sets up all the smart plugs

```
async function run() {
    try {
        await client.connect('opc.tcp://localhost:4840/UA/
        SmartPlugsServer');

        const session = await client.createSession();
        console.log('SmartPlug connected to Server');
        const subscription = opcua.ClientSubscription.
        create(session, {
            requestedPublishingInterval: 1000,
            requestedLifetimeCount: 10,
            requestedMaxKeepAliveCount: 2,
            maxNotificationsPerPublish: 10,
```

```
            publishingEnabled: true,
            priority: 10
        });

        subscription.on("started", () => {
            console.log('SmartPlug subscribed to server');
        });

        for (let plug of plugs) {
            setupDevice(session, subscription, plug);
        }
    }
    catch (e) {
        console.error('OPC UA error ' + e.message);
    }
}
```

All that is left to do is to import the plugs.json file as the global variable plugs and call the run() function. Listing 7-24 displays the whole driver file.

Listing 7-24. The smart plug driver modified to support several smart plugs

```
const opcua = require("node-opcua")
const client = opcua.OPCUAClient.create();

const plugs = require('../plugs.json');
const smart = require('./tplink_smartplug.js');

function writeValues(session, values) {
    let nodes = [];
    for (let valueData of values) {
        nodes.push({
            nodeId: valueData.nodeId,
```

```javascript
                attributeId: opcua.AttributeIds.Value,
                value: {
                    value: new opcua.Variant({
                        dataType: valueData.dataType,
                        value: valueData.value,
                        statusCode: opcua.StatusCodes.Good,
                    }),
                    sourceTimestamp: new Date()
                },
            });
        }
        return session.write(nodes);
}

function writeBadValues(session, nodeIds) {
    let nodes = [];
    for (let nodeId of nodeIds) {
        nodes.push({
            nodeId,
            attributeId: opcua.AttributeIds.Value,
            value: {
                statusCode: opcua.StatusCodes.Bad,
            },
            sourceTimestamp: new Date()
        });
    }
    return session.write(nodes);
}

async function setupDevice(session, subscription, plug) {
    const smartPlug = await subscription.monitor({ nodeId:
'ns=1;s=/SmartPower/' + plug.name + '/Actions/switch' },
```

```
    {
        samplingInterval: 500,
        discardOldest: true,
        queueSize: 1
    },
    opcua.TimestampsToReturn.Both);

smartPlug.on('changed', (data) => {
    if (data.statusCode === opcua.StatusCodes.Good) {
        if (data.value.value === true) {
            smart.on(plug.ip);
        }
        else {
            smart.off(plug.ip)
        }
    }
});

setInterval(async () => {
    try {
        let energy = await smart.readEnergy(plug.ip);
        if (energy.err_code === 0) {
            let values = [
                {
                    nodeId: 'ns=1;s=/SmartPower/' + plug.
                    name + '/Energy/voltage',
                    dataType: opcua.DataType.Float,
                    value: energy.voltage,
                },
                {
                    nodeId: 'ns=1;s=/SmartPower/' + plug.
                    name + '/Energy/current',
```

```
                        dataType: opcua.DataType.Float,
                        value: energy.current
                },
                {
                        nodeId: 'ns=1;s=/SmartPower/' + plug.
                        name + '/Energy/power',
                        dataType: opcua.DataType.Float,
                        value: energy.power
                }
            ];
            await writeValues(session, values);
        }
        else {
            let nodes = [
                'ns=1;s=/SmartPower/' + plug.name +
                '/Energy/voltage',
                'ns=1;s=/SmartPower/' + plug.name +
                '/Energy/current',
                'ns=1;s=/SmartPower/' + plug.name +
                '/Energy/power'
            ];
            await writeBadValues(session, nodes);
        }
    }
    catch (e) {
        console.error('OPC UA server energy write error ' +
        e.message);
    }
}, 3000);
```

```javascript
setInterval(async () => {
    try {
        let sysinfo = await smart.readSysinfo(plug.ip);
        if (sysinfo.err_code === 0) {
            let values = [
                {
                    nodeId: 'ns=1;s=/SmartPower/' + plug.
                    name + '/Sysinfo/alias',
                    dataType: opcua.DataType.String,
                    value: sysinfo.alias,
                },
                {
                    nodeId: 'ns=1;s=/SmartPower/' + plug.
                    name + '/Sysinfo/relay',
                    dataType: opcua.DataType.Boolean,
                    value: (sysinfo.relay_state === 1) ?
                    true : false,
                }
            ];
            await writeValues(session, values);
        }
        else {
            let nodes = [
                'ns=1;s=/SmartPower/' + plug.name +
                '/Sysinfo/relay'
            ];
            await writeBadValues(session, nodes);
        }
    }
```

```
        catch (e) {
            console.error('OPC UA server relay write error ' +
            e.message);
        }
    }, 3000);
}

async function run() {
    try {
        await client.connect('opc.tcp://localhost:4840/UA/
        SmartPlugsServer');

        const session = await client.createSession();
        console.log('SmartPlug connected to Server');
        const subscription = opcua.ClientSubscription.
        create(session, {
            requestedPublishingInterval: 1000,
            requestedLifetimeCount: 10,
            requestedMaxKeepAliveCount: 2,
            maxNotificationsPerPublish: 10,
            publishingEnabled: true,
            priority: 10
        });

        subscription.on("started", () => {
            console.log('SmartPlug subscribed to server');
        });

        for (let plug of plugs) {
            setupDevice(session, subscription, plug);
        }
    }
```

```
catch (e) {
    console.error('OPC UA error ' + e.message);
}
}
run();
```

To verify that the code works, we run the project and read the values using the ProSys OPC UA Client. We should be able to see the power values, the alias, and relay status and be able to switch the smart plug on and off by writing into the Actions/switch variable.

Store the Information in the Database

The next component of the project is data storage. The purpose of this component is to store information in the MariaDB database that we have set at the beginning of the chapter.

MariaDB uses usernames and passwords to authenticate and authorize access to databases and tables. The first step is to create a username and password for this component. The user has to have access to writing data to the meters and onoff tables. Let us run the MariaDB monitor. For this, we go to the SHELL tab and use the sudo mariadb command. This opens the MariaDB monitor. Next, we specify the database that we aim to manipulate (Listing 7-25).

Listing 7-25. The MariaDB monitor

```
pi@raspberrypi:~ $ sudo mariadb
Welcome to the MariaDB monitor.  Commands end with ; or \g.
Your MariaDB connection id is 594
Server version: 10.3.17-MariaDB-0+deb10u1 Raspbian 10

Copyright (c) 2000, 2018, Oracle, MariaDB Corporation Ab and
others.
```

```
Type 'help;' or '\h' for help. Type '\c' to clear the current
input statement.

MariaDB [(none)]> USE smartpower;
Database changed
MariaDB [smartpower]>
```

Next, we need to create a username and password. The CREATE USER command helps us do this. The user that we want to create is called *smartpowerwrite*, and the password is *smartpowerwrite*.

Note   The password is not really a security feature as MariaDB is not allowing any connections from outside the Raspberry Pi. As long as a user has access to the Raspberry Pi, we have access to MariaDB. The credentials are useful to prevent wrongful access due to software bugs.

After the user is created, we have to grant it INSERT, UPDATE, and SELECT rights into the tables of the smartpower database. We use the GRANT command, as shown in Listing 7-26.

Listing 7-26. Create a user and grant INSERT, UPDATE, and SELECT rights

```
MariaDB [smartpower]> CREATE USER smartpowerwrite IDENTIFIED BY
'smartpowerwrite';
Query OK, 0 rows affected (0.007 sec)

MariaDB [smartpower]> GRANT INSERT,UPDATE,SELECT ON
smartpower.* TO smartpowerwrite;
Query OK, 0 rows affected (0.001 sec)
```

Now we are ready to write data into the smartpower database. For this, inside the project folder, we need to create a new folder called **database** and, inside it, a file called **index.js**. To be able to access MariaDB from Node.js, we need to install the mariadb library. We use the *Package Manager* to do that.

Note   If installing the MariaDB package is not working via the Package Manager, you can run the following command in the shell: sudo npm install -g mariadb --unsafe-perm.

The database component works in the following way: it connects to the OPC UA Server and MariaDB server; at a fixed time interval, five seconds in our example, it reads the power and relay values for each smart plug from the OPC UA Server and writes them into the database. If a smart plug has an error, meaning the value of the status code in the OPC UA Server is set to Bad, the component writes NULL instead of an actual power value.

When it comes to the relay status, our onoff table stores one entry for each smart plug. The values of the relay field in the table have the following meaning:

- 0 – The smart plug is switched on.

- 1 – The smart plug is switched off.

- 2 – The smart plug has an error.

The first step in writing the database component is to import the libraries. We import the OPC UA library, the MariaDB library, and the plugs. json file (Listing 7-27). After importing the libraries, we create a MariaDB connection pool. This is related to MariaDB's library.

Listing 7-27. Set up the connection to MariaDB

```
const opcua = require('node-opcua')
const client = opcua.OPCUAClient.create();

const plugs = require ('../plugs.json');

const mariadb = require('mariadb');
const pool = mariadb.createPool({host: '127.0.0.1',
user: 'smartpowerwrite', password: 'smartpowerwrite',
connectionLimit: 5});
```

MariaDB and MySQL were designed to power the Web. The language that was mostly used at that time for writing web applications was PHP. The PHP language has a particular way in which it works: each time that a user loads a PHP page in the browser, the web server executes the PHP script, captures all its output (mostly print functions writing HTML), and sends it to the browser. This means that the PHP program is run every time a user accesses a PHP page, it prints out some HTML and then stops. What this means for the database connection is that each time a page is loaded, the PHP library connects to the database, sends the queries, and disconnects. MariaDB and MySQL are optimized for fast and short time connections.

Our application works differently, though. It is not designed to start and stop frequently; it is programmed to never stop. Due to this, it should connect to the database when it starts and never disconnect. The issue is that the database system is not optimized for this kind of behavior. To solve this, the Node.js library uses a connection pool. This means that the library automatically handles the connections to the database and handles connection errors. A connection pool is created using the `createPool()` function. It receives an object as argument having the following properties:

- *host* – The address of the MariaDB database, for our project the localhost address

- *user* – The username to use for the connection

- *password* – The password to use for the username

- *connectionLimit* – The maximum number of connections that are available

Every time the application wants to access the MariaDB database, it requests a connection from the connection pool. When the application is done with reading or writing from the database, it disconnects. From the programmer's point of view, this is just like using MariaDB in a PHP program. On the other hand, the MariaDB library connection pool handles the actual connections, starting and closing connections when needed.

Note   The createPool() function does not yet connect to the MariaDB database, but stores the properties.

Now that we have a database connection pool setup, we can define the data storage functions. The first function we define is energyMonitor() (Listing 7-28). This starts a timer so that every five seconds, it queries the OPC UA Server for the energy values and writes them into the MariaDB database. We want to read the data from the OPC UA Server every five seconds, even if the data has not changed. We use the read() function for this. It is similar to the write() function, just that instead of writing data to the OPC UA Server, it reads data from it. The function receives an array of variables IDs and returns an array of variable values.

Listing 7-28. The function that monitors the power values

```
function energyMonitor (session, deviceName)
{
    setInterval (async () => {
        let values = await session.read ([
            {nodeId: 'ns=1;s=/SmartPower/'+deviceName+'/Energy/
            voltage'},
```

```
        {nodeId: 'ns=1;s=/SmartPower/'+deviceName+'/Energy/
        current'},
        {nodeId: 'ns=1;s=/SmartPower/'+deviceName+'/Energy/
        power'}
]);
let writeValues = [];
for (let valueData of values)
{
    if (valueData.statusCode === opcua.StatusCodes.Good)
    {
        writeValues.push (valueData.value.value);
    }
    else
    {
        writeValues.push (null);
    }
}
let dbconnection = await pool.getConnection();
if (dbconnection !== null)
{
    try
    {
        await dbconnection.query('USE smartpower;');
        await dbconnection.query('INSERT INTO meters
        SET smartplug="'+deviceName+'", voltage=?,
        current=?, power=?;', writeValues);
    }
    catch (e)
    {
        console.error ('energy: '+e.message);
    }
```

```
}
  await dbconnection.close ();
}, 5000);
```

If the read is successful, we need to write the data to the database. First, we need to get a connection from the MariaDB connection pool using the getConnection() function. If there is a connection available, it returns it. Otherwise, null is returned. The second step is the database selection. In MariaDB, tables are grouped in databases. When we designed our data model, we created a database called smartpower. To use any tables, we first have to select the database. This is done using the USE keyword followed by the name of the database's name, in our case, smartpower.

The next query is one inserting data. We use the INSERT INTO query. The INSERT syntax is shown in Listing 7-29.

Listing 7-29. The INSERT INTO query syntax

```
INSERT INTO table_name SET field=value,
anotherfield=anothervalue, ...;
```

Tip   Each MariaDB connection has one active database at a time. The database can be changed at any time using the USE keyword.

To send a query to the database, we use the query() function. This receives two parameters: the query in the form of a string and an array of values. You might ask why this is necessary; we could have written the whole query in the string (including the values). The answer is: for security reasons, to avoid SQL injection. This way, inside the query, we can place ? instead of the actual values. Each ? is replaced with the escaped value from the array.

Note   Escaped value means the value in a way that it can be written as a string. For example, if the value that you want to write has ", this needs to be rewritten as \".

The next function we have to define is `relayMonitor()` (Listing 7-30). This function writes the status of the smart plug into the database. Here we write one of the three values:

- 0 – If the relay is on.

- 1 – If the relay is off.

- 2 – If the smart plug is not working or offline.

The difference between this table and the table storing the power values is that this table stores only one entry for each smart plug. The fields of the table have the following meaning:

- *timestamp* – The date and time of the latest update.

- *smartplug* – The name of the smart plug.

- *relay* – The state of the smart plug (0, 1, or 2).

Listing 7-30. The function that monitors the relay

```
async function relayMonitor (session, deviceName)
{
    setInterval (async () => {
        let values = await session.read ([
            {nodeId: 'ns=1;s=/SmartPower/'+deviceName+
            '/Sysinfo/relay'},
        ]);
        let valueData = values[0];
        let value = 2;
```

```
    if (valueData.statusCode === opcua.StatusCodes.Good)
    {
        value = valueData.value.value?0:1;
    }
    let dbconnection = await pool.getConnection();
    if (dbconnection !== null)
    {
        try
        {
            await dbconnection.query('USE smartpower;');
            await dbconnection.query('INSERT INTO onoff
            SET smartplug="'+deviceName+'", relay=? ON
            DUPLICATE KEY UPDATE relay=?, timestamp=?',
            [value, value, new Date()]);
        }
        catch (e)
        {
            console.error ('relay: '+e.message);
        }
    }
    await dbconnection.close ();
}, 3000);
```

The relayMonitor() function queries the Sysinfo/relay variable
from the OPC UA Server for each smart plug every five seconds and
updates the row for that smart plug in the table. The query to update the
data is a bit more complex (and dependent on MariaDB). We want to use
one single query to either insert new values if there is no row for that smart
plug, or update values if there is a row for that smart plug. For this, we use
the INSERT INTO query with the parameter ON DUPLICATE KEY UPDATE.
The whole query is shown in Listing 7-31.

Listing 7-31. Insert or update a row in a table

```
INSERT INTO table_name VALUES field=value, ... ON DUPLICATE KEY
UPDATE field=value, ...;
```

This query works as follows: it tries to insert in the table a new row. If there is another row that has the same value for the primary key field, the insert fails (the primary key field must have a unique value for each row). If the insert fails due to this, the ON DUPLICATE KEY UPDATE instructs MariaDB to update the following fields' values instead of inserting a new row. Using this query, we make sure that there is only one row for each smart plug (the smartplug field is the primary key) and that the row's data is updated every time. Were it not for this, we would have had to build a transaction where we first tried to select the row for the smart plug, and if it works, update the row, or if it does not work, insert a new one.

We now have all the functions necessary for reading the values from the OPC UA Server and writing them to the MariaDB database. All that is left to do is to modify the run() function. This connects to the OPC UA Server and runs the two functions for writing data to the database. Listing 7-32 displays the complete source code.

Listing 7-32. The database component

```
const opcua = require('node-opcua')
const client = opcua.OPCUAClient.create();

const plugs = require ('../plugs.json');
const mariadb = require('mariadb');

const pool = mariadb.createPool({host: '192.168.0.1',
user: 'smartpowerwrite', password: 'smartpowerwrite',
connectionLimit: 5});
```

```
function energyMonitor (session, deviceName)
{
    setInterval (async () => {
        let values = await session.read ([
            {nodeId: 'ns=1;s=/SmartPower/'+deviceName+'/Energy/
            voltage'},
            {nodeId: 'ns=1;s=/SmartPower/'+deviceName+'/Energy/
            current'},
            {nodeId: 'ns=1;s=/SmartPower/'+deviceName+'/Energy/
            power'}
        ]);
        let writeValues = [];
        for (let valueData of values)
        {
            if (valueData.statusCode === opcua.StatusCodes.Good)
            {
                writeValues.push (valueData.value.value);
            }
            else
            {
                writeValues.push (null);
            }
        }
        let dbconnection = await pool.getConnection();
        if (dbconnection !== null)
        {
            try
            {
                await dbconnection.query('USE smartpower;');
                await dbconnection.query('INSERT INTO meters
                SET smartplug="'+deviceName+'", voltage=?,
                current=?, power=?;', writeValues);
            }
```

```
            catch (e)
            {
                console.error ('energy: '+e.message);
            }
        }
        await dbconnection.close ();
    }, 5000);
}

async function relayMonitor (session, deviceName)
{
    setInterval (async () => {
        let values = await session.read ([
            {nodeId: 'ns=1;s=/SmartPower/'+deviceName+'/
            Sysinfo/relay'},
        ]);
        let valueData = values[0];
        let value = 2;
        if (valueData.statusCode === opcua.StatusCodes.Good)
        {
            value = valueData.value.value?0:1;
        }
        let dbconnection = await pool.getConnection();
        if (dbconnection !== null)
        {
            try
            {
                await dbconnection.query('USE smartpower;');
                await dbconnection.query('INSERT INTO onoff
                SET smartplug="'+deviceName+'", relay=? ON
                DUPLICATE KEY UPDATE relay=?, timestamp=?',
                [value, value, new Date()]);
            }
```

```
            catch (e)
            {
                console.error ('relay: '+e.message);
            }
        }
        await dbconnection.close ();
    }, 3000);
}

async function run ()
{
    try
    {
        await client.connect ('opc.tcp://localhost:4840/UA/
        SmartPlugsServer');

        const session = await client.createSession();
        console.log ('database connected to Server');

        for (let plug of plugs)
        {
            energyMonitor (session, plug.name);
            relayMonitor (session, plug.name);
        }
    }
    catch (e)
    {
        console.error ('OPC UA error '+e.message);
    }
}

run ();
```

Now, let us import the database component in the **main.js** file, and our application is ready to be run. Listing 7-33 displays the complete **main.js** file.

Listing 7-33. The main.js file

```
// start the OPC/UA server
require ('./server');

// start the power plug driver driver
require ('./driver');

// start the database and write data
require ('./database');
```

All that is left is to run the project. To verify that it works, we display the data from the meters and onoff tables using the MariaDB monitor. For this, we use the SELECT query (Figure 7-8).

```
[MariaDB [(none)]> USE smartpower;
Reading table information for completion of table and column names
You can turn off this feature to get a quicker startup with -A

Database changed
[MariaDB [smartpower]> SELECT * FROM meters;
+-------+---------------------+-----------+---------+----------+---------+
| id    | timestamp           | smartplug | voltage | current  | power   |
+-------+---------------------+-----------+---------+----------+---------+
| 11267 | 2019-11-22 17:29:02 | SmartPlug1 |   NULL  |    NULL  |   NULL  |
| 11268 | 2019-11-22 17:29:02 | SmartPlug2 | 220.321 | 0.011975 |     0   |
| 11269 | 2019-11-22 17:29:07 | SmartPlug1 |   NULL  |    NULL  |   NULL  |
| 11270 | 2019-11-22 17:29:07 | SmartPlug2 | 220.196 | 0.020179 | 1.98773 |
| 11271 | 2019-11-22 17:29:12 | SmartPlug1 |   NULL  |    NULL  |   NULL  |
| 11272 | 2019-11-22 17:29:12 | SmartPlug2 |  220.08 | 0.019649 |  1.8102 |
| 11273 | 2019-11-22 17:30:48 | SmartPlug1 | 219.472 | 0.012628 |     0   |
| 11274 | 2019-11-22 17:30:48 | SmartPlug2 | 219.625 | 0.012023 |     0   |
| 11275 | 2019-11-22 17:30:53 | SmartPlug1 | 219.936 | 0.012539 |     0   |
| 11276 | 2019-11-22 17:30:53 | SmartPlug2 | 220.142 | 0.012185 |     0   |
| 11277 | 2019-11-22 17:30:59 | SmartPlug1 |  219.97 | 0.012496 |     0   |
| 11278 | 2019-11-22 17:30:59 | SmartPlug2 | 220.207 |  0.01216 |     0   |
| 11279 | 2019-11-22 17:31:03 | SmartPlug1 | 219.879 |  0.01278 |     0   |
| 11280 | 2019-11-22 17:31:03 | SmartPlug2 | 220.124 | 0.012185 |     0   |
+-------+---------------------+-----------+---------+----------+---------+
14 rows in set (0.001 sec)

[MariaDB [smartpower]> SELECT * FROM onoff;
+---------------------+-----------+-------+
| timestamp           | smartplug | relay |
+---------------------+-----------+-------+
| 2019-11-22 17:31:43 | SmartPlug1 |    1 |
| 2019-11-22 17:31:43 | SmartPlug2 |    1 |
+---------------------+-----------+-------+
2 rows in set (0.000 sec)
```

Figure 7-8. *Querying the MariaDB tables*

In the listed tables, you can see that there are values for both of the smart plugs in the meters table, and there is one row for each smart plug in the onoff table.

Summary

In this chapter, we have described how to read data from several smart plugs and store it in a MariaDB database. As the SD card used by the Raspberry Pi is not a reliable storage media, we have attached an external storage system to the Raspberry Pi and have configured MariaDB to store the databases on this external storage.

We also used a power over Ethernet HAT, so the device is not dependent on a power source. This way, we managed to build our application while highlighting industrial technologies.

CHAPTER 8

Data Plotting

One of the biggest advantages of IoT system is their autonomy and self-reliance. The ambient intelligence typical of IoT systems is achieved by removing human operators from the loop whenever possible. For example, machine-to-machine (M2M) communications establishes direct communications between IoT devices to exchange data, information, and to perform actions in a synchronized manner.

While modern IoT system should be "invisible", that is, they should not bother the user/customer for feedback or approval, there are situations where a dashboard or control board for interactions with human users should be provided. In these cases, the interface to the IoT system should be as simple and as friendly as possible in order not to confuse or discourage the consumer from using it. As such, considerable effort is being dedicated to the setup of data processing and plotting pipelines for IoT data.

An important part of any IoT system is data manipulation. This refers to programming the sensors so we can gather data, process it, and extract the information that we are interested in (e.g., the number of people in a picture). The next step is to store that information so we can access it anytime. Finally, we need to find a way of displaying the data to the user. Since printing a list of values on the screen is not very intuitive and user-friendly, we use a plotting system.

© Ioana Culic; Alexandru Radovici; Cristian Rusu 2020
I. Culic et al., *Commercial and Industrial Internet of Things Applications with the Raspberry Pi*,
https://doi.org/10.1007/978-1-4842-5296-3_8

In the previous chapter, we have built a system that stores data about the smart power plugs in a database, thus making the system persistent. In this chapter, we aim to take this project further and integrate it with a professional plotting system called Grafana.[1]

Necessary Components

The setup necessary for this project is the same one as from the previous chapter. We use the same components to store data in the MariaDB database and then plot this data to graphs.

Getting Started

The purpose of this chapter is to extend the application we have previously built, so the data we collected is displayed using visual widgets. Therefore, we start from the previously created application.

As this application has the data collection and storage in place, the next step is to plot it using a dashboard system. For this, we use Grafana, an open source dashboard system licensed under Apache 2.0. This means that anyone can use it without paying royalties.

Note   While using Grafana for free is an advantage, we suggest looking at a support plan for commercial applications.

First, we need to install Grafana. We can do this by using the docker container system and adding MariaDB as a data source.

---

[1]https://grafana.com

Install Docker

The easiest way to install Grafana is by using a container image. Container images are applications that come with all the necessary library stack to run. For instance, if we want to install a piece of software on a computer, it depends on some software libraries. Moreover, usually, it depends on a Linux distribution like Ubuntu or Fedora. This causes many issues when installing software, as some of the libraries that are installed might have been updated since the software was compiled by its vendor. Most of the time, system administrators have to compile the software on the computer that they want it installed on. Containers solve this issue by shipping a piece of software with all the necessary libraries.

Think of a container image as a *virtual machine (VM)*, except that the container shares the operating system (kernel) with the host. In other words, the software that is shipped as a container uses only the operating system, all other dependencies being inside the container. In this way, all you need to run a Linux application that comes in a container is the container system (to be able to start the container) and any Linux that has containers support.

One of the most used container systems is docker. This is what we are also using for Grafana. The first step is to install docker on the Raspberry Pi. For this, we open a SHELL tab and run the following command: `curl -sSL https://get.docker.com | sh`.

The installation takes a few minutes. After it is ready, we can run the `docker` command in the shell. Usually, only the `root` user has access to the container system. The next step is to add the regular user, `pi`, to the `docker` group so we can use the `docker` command without running `sudo`. Listing 8-1 shows how we can do this. We have to restart the shell for the new group changes to take effect. We use the `exit` command and press any key to start the shell.

Listing 8-1. Add the user pi to the docker group to run the docker command without sudo

```
pi@raspberrypi:~ $ sudo usermod -aG docker pi
pi@raspberrypi:~ $ exit
```

To verify that our docker installation works, we run a simple container that prints hello world. Listing 8-2 shows the command and the print from hello-world.

Listing 8-2. Test docker installation

```
pi@raspberrypi:~ $ docker run hello-world
Unable to find image 'hello-world:latest' locally
latest: Pulling from library/hello-world
c1eda109e4da: Pull complete
Digest: sha256:c3b4ada4687bbaa170745b3e4dd8ac3f194ca95b2d0518b4
17fb47e5879d9b5f
Status: Downloaded newer image for hello-world:latest

Hello from Docker!
This message shows that your installation appears to be working
correctly.
To generate this message, Docker took the following steps:
 1. The Docker client contacted the Docker daemon.
 2. The Docker daemon pulled the "hello-world" image from the
Docker Hub.
    (arm32v7)
 3. The Docker daemon created a new container from that image
which runs the
    executable that produces the output you are currently reading.
 4. The Docker daemon streamed that output to the Docker
client, which sent it
    to your terminal.
```

To try something more ambitious, you can run an Ubuntu container with:

```
$ docker run -it ubuntu bash
```

Share images, automate workflows, and more with a free Docker ID:

https://hub.docker.com/

For more examples and ideas, visit:

https://docs.docker.com/get-started/

Note   Container images are automatically downloaded from Docker Hub. When you want to run a container whose image is not present locally, docker will download the image and run the container afterward.

Install Grafana

The first step to take when installing Grafana is to create a folder where its configuration data is stored. Grafana does not store data, it stores the dashboards (the graphs we use and the settings for these graphs), the data sources that are configured (credentials to MariaDB), and other plugins that we might install. We create a folder on the external storage (the /**storage**/**smartdata** folder). We name the folder **grafana** and make the user **pi** its owner (Listing 8-3).

Listing 8-3. Create the grafana folder

```
pi@raspberrypi:~ $ sudo mkdir /storage/smartpower/grafana
pi@raspberrypi:~ $ sudo chown pi:pi /storage/smartpower/grafana
```

Note   If you are not using an external storage, you can create a folder anywhere on the Raspberry Pi.

Before we start Grafana, we have to create a connection between the Raspberry Pi and the Grafana container. This is done by creating a private network. For that, we use the docker network create command and create a network called smartpowernet. We create a network just like the one shown in Figure 8-1. The commands are illustrated in Listing 8-4.

Listing 8-4. Create a private docker network

```
pi@raspberrypi:~ $ docker network create --gateway
192.168.120.1 --subnet 192.168.120.0/24 smartpowernet
ae75c049f13a03721bd33fdf05f125214ee8ca3332e3d6d2c7d9d536488e61d6
pi@raspberrypi:~ $ docker network ls
NETWORK ID            NAME              DRIVER       SCOPE
e2ccf753cf91   bridge            bridge       local
1619b800af7f   host              host         local
20d4088148c7   none              null         local
ae75c049f13a   smartpowernet     bridge       local
```

The new network has the Raspberry Pi as a gateway to the Internet, having the IP address 192.168.120.1, a virtual switch that is managed by docker, and a host that is the Grafana container. The IP address of the container is any available address in the same network.

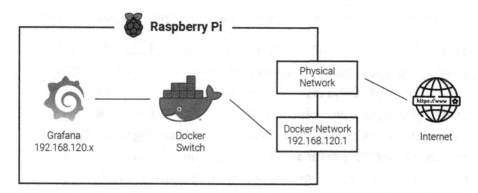

Figure 8-1. *The smartpowernet network*

Using the `docker network ls` command, we can list the available networks. If the `smartpowernet` network shows up, everything worked OK. Now, let us run Grafana (Listing 8-5). The commands that we run perform the following operations:

- Download the Grafana container image from Docker Hub.

- Start the image.

- Download two dashboard plugins (*vonage-status-panel* and *grafana-clock-panel*).

- Set Grafana to run at the Raspberry Pi boot (when docker starts).

- Use the **/storage/smartpower/grafana** folder.

- Use port 3000 for the web interface.

Listing 8-5. Install and run Grafana with plugins and storage space

```
pi@raspberrypi:~ $ sudo docker run   --user=$UID -d --restart
always  -p 3000:3000  --name=grafana  -e "GF_SERVER_ROOT_
URL=http://192.168.1.47" -e "GF_INSTALL_PLUGINS=vonage-
status-panel,grafana-clock-panel"  -e "GF_SECURITY_ADMIN_
PASSWORD=secret" --net smartpowernet -v /storage/smartpower/
grafana:/var/lib/grafana  grafana/grafana:6.3.6
Unable to find image 'grafana/grafana:6.3.6' locally
6.3.6: Pulling from grafana/grafana
245dbad35e84: Pull complete
bc1d94e06384: Pull complete
1578a1c7d8ec: Pull complete
d5d560aa8fbb: Pull complete
525bba436572: Pull complete
b5d3581c6846: Pull complete
11664e74e734: Pull complete
2b25cb5ab71f: Pull complete
70952cf6efd0: Pull complete
Digest: sha256:218ba67bfac261a71abde7cb306727edaa7d9a595bd70ceb
5a644ea3dfb21229
Status: Downloaded newer image for grafana/grafana:6.3.6
78e3616b8df91d2e088e23a931a858a5fef6be3f677a2d8781e4a761edb9045d
pi@raspberrypi:~ $ docker ps
CONTAINER ID  IMAGE    COMMAND  CREATED  STATUS   PORTS    NAMES
78e3616b8df9   grafana/grafana:6.3.6  "/run.sh"      24
seconds ago  Up 6 seconds  0.0.0.0:3000->3000/tcp   grafana
```

To verify if Grafana is working, we use the docker ps command. This displays all the running containers.

Note   Please replace the items in bold in Listing 8-5 with your parameters: the IP address of your Raspberry Pi, a desired password (ours is the word **secret**), and the folder to store Grafana's data.

We can log in into Grafana's UI and start building the dashboard. We use a web browser and go to the http://192.168.1.47:3000 address. Please replace the IP with your Raspberry Pi's IP address. A login screen similar to the one in Figure 8-2 should appear.

Note   Use the **admin** username and the password that you used when starting Grafana. In our example, the password is the word **secret**.

Figure 8-2. *Grafana login screen*

Add the MariaDB Data Source

The next step is to connect MariaDB to Grafana. First, we configure MariaDB to listen to the smartpowernet network interface. By default, MariaDB is listening for connections only on the 127.0.0.1 interface, to disallow any connections from outside. Thus, we have to edit the **/etc/mysql/mariadb.conf.d/50-server.cnf** file and change the bind-address property to 192.168.120.1 (Listing 8-6). Save the file with the new value and restart MariaDB using the following shell command: sudo systemctl start mariadb.

Listing 8-6. MariaDB listen address

```
# Instead of skip-networking the default is now to #listen only on
# localhost which is more compatible and is not less #secure.

bind-address            = 192.168.120.1
```

Note   Even if we changed the IP address that MariaDB listens on to a network address different from localhost, connections from outside the Raspberry Pi do not work, as the new IP address is on a virtual network inside the Raspberry Pi.

The next step is to create a user for Grafana. This user has to be able to read data from the smartpower database tables. We use the CREATE USER and GRANT commands, similar to the way we created the user for the database component (Listing 8-7).

Listing 8-7. Create the smartpowerread user and grant the SELECT right

```
MariaDB [(none)]> USE smartpower;
Reading table information for completion of table and column names
You can turn off this feature to get a quicker startup with -A

Database changed
MariaDB [smartpower]> CREATE USER smartpowerread IDENTIFIED BY
'smartpowerread';
Query OK, 0 rows affected (0.001 sec)

MariaDB [smartpower]> GRANT SELECT ON smartpower.* TO
smartpowerread;
Query OK, 0 rows affected (0.001 sec)
```

Now that MariaDB is accessible from within the Grafana container, let us set up the data source. After logging in to Grafana, you should get the *Home Dashboard*. Go to the *Add data source* option and select *MySQL* as a new data source. Figure 8-3 shows the *Home Dashboard*.

Note   MariaDB is compatible with MySQL.

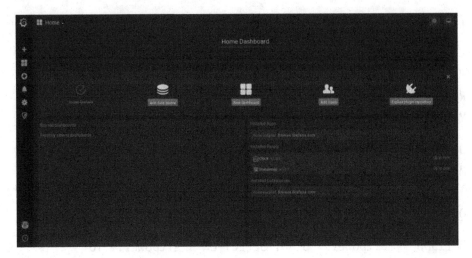

Figure 8-3. *Grafana home dashboard*

In the *data source* options, we fill out the hostname with *192.168.120.1*, the database name with *smartpower*, the username with *smartpowerrea*d, and the password with *smartpowerread* (Figure 8-4). To save the data source, scroll to the bottom, and click *Save & Test*. If everything is OK, there should be a message showing *Database Connection OK*.

MySQL Connection

Host	192.168.120.1
Database	smartpower
User	nartpowerread Password ··············
TLS Client Auth	☐ With CA Cert 🛈 ☐
Skip TLS Verify	☐

Figure 8-4. *Grafana MariaDB data source setup*

There is another step we have to take, that is to change the host address of MariaDB inside our project's database component. Go to **database/index.js** and change the MariaDB connection pool address from 127.0.0.1 to 192.168.120.1. We have to restart our project.

The Dashboard

Now, it is time to design the dashboard. For this, we go to the *Home Dashboard* by clicking the upper left icon in Grafana. From the *Home Dashboard*, we select *New dashboard*. This creates an empty dashboard that we can edit (Figure 8-5).

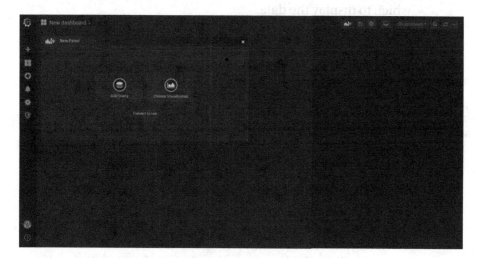

Figure 8-5. *Grafana empty dashboard*

Let us go over the interface of the new dashboard. In the top left corner, we have the name, in this case, *New dashboard*. On the top right side, we have the following buttons:

- Add panel – This adds a panel similar to the one displayed in the new dashboard.

- Save dashboard – This allows us to save any changes that we make to the dashboard.

- Dashboard settings – This allows us to set some properties of the dashboard, like the name or the data refresh rate (the interval at which new data is read from the database and displayed on the dashboard).

- Cycle view mode – This allows us to change the way the dashboard is displayed, cycling between edit mode, viewing mode, and full-screen mode.

- A dropdown that allows us to select the time span in which to display the data.

- A dropdown that allows us to select the data refresh rate quickly.

Now let us add our first widget. We add the clock. For this, we select *Choose Visualization* from the *New Panel*. This takes us to the widget screen shown in Figure 8-6. On the left side, there are three round buttons:

- Queries – This allows us to create a database query.

- Visualization – This allows us to select the widget type and set its properties (this is the button that is selected in Figure 8-6).

- General – This allows us to set properties related to the panel, for example, its name.

Note   Grafana calls the graphs widgets.

Figure 8-6. *New widget screen with the clock widget type selected*

In the *Visualization* tab, we select the *Clock* widget. This widget does not depend on any data from the database; it just displays the current time. In the *General* tab, we can change the name of the panel to *Time*. To go back to the dashboard, we click the back arrow shown next to the dashboard title (upper left corner).

In the dashboard page, we can now resize the clock panel so that it takes less space. To resize a panel, click the lower right corner and start dragging.

Now that we have our first widget, let us save the dashboard; otherwise, it will be lost whenever Grafana (or the Raspberry Pi) is restarted. We just have to click the *Save dashboard* button in the upper right corner and give the dashboard a name. We use *SmartPower*.

The next step is to add the instant power values. This means adding a gauge for each smart plug that displays the voltage, current, and power. For this, we add a new panel and select *Add query*. Now we have to add a database query to retrieve data. For this widget, we want to get the *voltage* value from the *meters* table. Grafana allows us to create the query in a graphic editor shown in Figure 8-7. We have to complete the fields shown in Table 8-1.

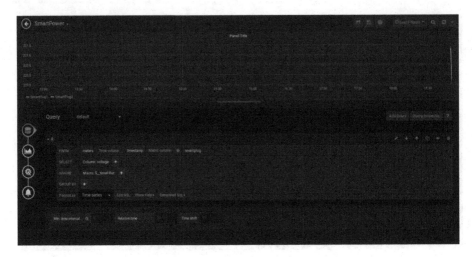

Figure 8-7. *Create the SQL query*

Table 8-1. *The Grafana query*

Field	Description	Value
From	The name of the table that we want to use.	meters
Time column	The name of the field in the selected table that stores the timestamp.	timestamp
Metric column	A widget can display several items. Grafana supposes that all the values are stored in one single table that has at least two fields: one storing the name of the value and one storing the actual value. In our case, we store all the three values in one row (voltage, current, and power) but have one field storing the name of the smart plug where the values come from. We use that field.	smartplug
Select	We can add several fields with values. In our case, we add the voltage field.	voltage

Next, let us select the widget type. In the *Visualization* tab, we can select *Gauge*, as shown in Figure 8-8. For this widget, we have to set several properties:

- Calc – The way the displayed value is calculated; we use Last to display the most recent value.

- Unit – The units displayed next to the value, we use Volt;

- Min – The minimum value; we use 0.

- Max – The maximum value; we use 250 (in Europe the power is at 230V; use 140V if you are in the United States).

- Thresholds – This allows us to set color ranges; set the red color at values higher than 240 (other value should be used for the United States).

Figure 8-8. *The gauge widget*

The next step is to select the *General* tab and set the panel's name to *Voltage*. We can now click the back arrow and go back to the dashboard. Feel free to move the new panel around and resize it.

To make sure that our dashboard will not be deleted when the Raspberry Pi restarts, we click *Save dashboard*.

Now, in a similar manner, we can add widgets for the *current* values and *power* values, the only difference being the field that is selected for the query, the range values, and the unit.

Similarly, we can add graphs that show the variation in time for the power values. Instead of selecting a gauge as visualization, we select a graph. All the other parameters are similar.

There is another important widget that we want to add: the smart plug's status. For each smart plug, we add a widget that displays a green square if the smart plug is on, an orange square if the smart plug is off, and a red square if the smart plug is not available or offline. We go over the steps for adding the first widget, the others being similar.

First, we add a new panel and select *Add Query*. We select the *onoff* table; the metric field is *smartplug*, and the value field is *relay*. The query is shown in Figure 8-9. In the *Visualization* tab, we select the *Status Panel* (Figure 8-10). This has the following properties:

- Alias – The name of the smart plug to display.

- Threshold – The values at which the status panel changes colors:

  - At values greater or equal to 1 it displays orange.

  - At values greater or equal to 2 it displays red.

  - At values lower than 1 it displays green.

- Display Alias – We instruct the status panel to always display the name of the smart plug.

- Display Value – We instruct the status panel to always display the value of the smart plug status (0, 1, or 2).

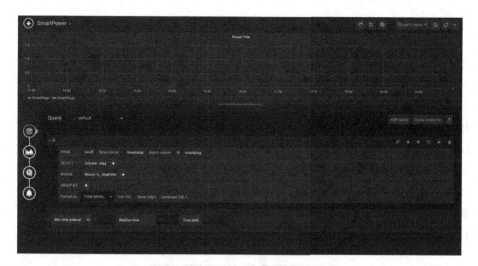

Figure 8-9. *The relay query*

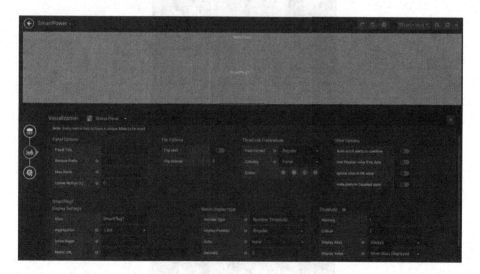

Figure 8-10. *The status panel*

In the *General* tab, we set the name of the panel to the name of the smart plug. Next, we click the back arrow and position and resize the status panel on the dashboard. The last step is to save the dashboard.

283

Note   Repeat the steps described earlier for every smart plug.

The last step we have to take is to set the dashboard's refresh rate. This is the interval at which the dashboard reads new data from the database. By default, this interval is set to *Off*, which means you have to refresh it manually. To set a new refresh rate, we click the dropdown in the upper right corner, just as it is shown in Figure 8-11. For a small value, the data updates more often, but the processing power consumption of the Raspberry Pi is higher. We suggest setting the refresh rate depending on the usage of the dashboard.

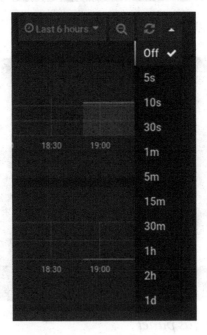

Figure 8-11. *The refresh rate*

Summary

In this chapter, we have extended the previously created application so we can display data using visual graphs. For this, we installed the Grafana dashboard software using docker containers and set it up to use MariaDB.

We have created the dashboard shown in Figure 8-12 to monitor the smart plug power values and status.

The system we developed is an appropriate option to monitor the power consumption in a small factory or office environment.

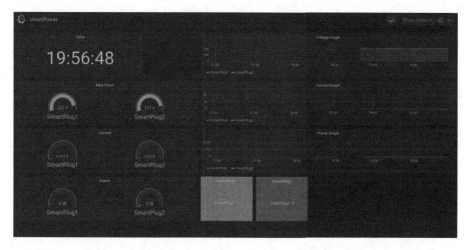

Figure 8-12. *The dashboard of the smart plug monitoring system*

Index

A

Advertisement system
    advantages, 125
    camera module
        configuration, 131, 132
        connection, 129, 130
    cognitive services
        account type selection, 138
        authentication keys, 139
        platform window, 137
        retrieve account keys, 138
    components, 127, 128
    content personalization,
        142–145
    Google service account
        (*see* Google Drive)
    monitor system
        motion sensor, 156
        PIR connection
            schematic, 157
    picture process
        Azure package
            header, 140
        raspistill command, 141
    update source pictures, 145
    USB camera connection, 155, 156

B

Bluetooth Low Energy (BLE), 25

C

Communications protocols
    application-level protocols
        CoAP, 27
        lower-level protocols, 26
        MQTT packets, 27
    low-level data transmission
        (*see* Low-level data
            transmission protocols)
Constraint Application Protocol
    (CoAP), 27

D

Data storage/processing
    database
        components, 249
        database component, 258–261

Application-level protocols
    CoAP, 27
    lower-level protocols, 26
    MQTT packets, 27

© Ioana Culic; Alexandru Radovici; Cristian Rusu 2020

I. Culic et al., *Commercial and Industrial Internet of Things Applications with the Raspberry Pi*,
https://doi.org/10.1007/978-1-4842-5296-3

Data storage/processing (*cont.*)
  INSERT INTO query
    syntax, 255
  INSERT/UPDATE/SELECT
    command, 250
  insert/update option, 258
  MariaDB monitor, 249
  SELECT query, 262, 263
  setup connection, 252
  table meaning, 256
external storage system, 211
IoT systems, 209
MariaDB-store data
  database systems, 211, 212
  data model setup, 223–227
  external storage setup,
    214–223
  installation, 213, 214
OPC UA data model, 229
Raspberry Pi PoE HAT, 210
smart plug driver
  data source code, 238–242
  properties, 236
smart plugs
  plugs.json, 229
  software architecture, 228
Digital signage system, 69
  advantages, 70
  building application
    Electron, 72
    GTK+/Qt/web-based
      libraries, 71
  components, 70, 71

modern electronics/software
  components, 70
pollution level, 69
Docker installation, 267–269

E, F

Edge computing
  advantages of, 17
  cloud processing/storage
    capabilities, 16
  Raspberry Pi
    device model, 17–19
    programmable logic
      controller, 20–22
    sensors/connected devices, 17
Electronic Logging Device
  (ELD/E-Log), 16
Ethernet/IP, 24

G, H

General Data Protection
  Regulation (GDPR), 126
Google Drive
  authentication key, 147
  integrate application, 150
    download/store picture
      contents, 152
    interaction, 151
    retrieves pictures, 152–154
  key creation, 148
  project creation, 146

service account, 145, 147
upload files
   files, 148
   get file ID, 150
   share image file, 149
   spreadsheet, 150
Grafana
  dashboard
    buttons, 277
    empty dashboard, 277
    gauge widget, 281
    properties, 281, 282
    query option, 280
    refresh rate, 284
    relay query, 283
    SQL query
     creation, 279, 280
    status panel, 283
    Visualization tab, 278, 279
    widget screen, 279
  folder creation, 269
  home dashboard, 276
  installation, 266, 269
  login screen, 273
  MariaDB, 274–277
  operations, 271
  plugins/storage space, 272
  private docker network, 270
  smart plug monitoring
    system, 285
  smartpowernet
    network, 271
Graphical user interface (GUI), 29

I, J, K

Industrial Internet of Things (IIoT)
  certification process, 12
  characteristics of, 8
  commercial/industrial
    environments, 14–16
  digital twins, 14
  edge intelligence, 15
  description, 3
  operational efficiency, 9
  prototyping system, 12–15
  requirements, 9
  SCADA systems, 10, 11
Industrial system
  advantages, 164
  architecture, 165–167
  components, 166
  OPC UA server (*see* Open Platform
    Communication – Unified
    Architecture (OPC UA))
  power plug driver
    energy values, 194–200
    error checking, 197
    monitor variable
     parameters, 204
    project structure, 176
    smart power GUI, 205, 206
  sensing/monitoring, 163
  smart plug system
    architecture, 168
    Kasa phone app, 169
    Python SDK, 169–175

Industrial system (*cont.*)

    smart power plug system
        architecture, 167

Integrated development
    environment (IDE), 50

Interface platform, 30

    libraries, 31

    REST API, 31, 32

Inter-Integrated
    Circuit (I^2C/I2C), 23

    get online data, 87

Internet Engineering Task Force
    (IETF), 2

Internet of Things (IoT)

    architecture, 6–8

    building system, 5

    characteristics of, 3–6

    commercial/industrial
        systems, 1

    communications
        protocols, 22–29

    data collection, 4

    design components, 45, 46

    dynamism, 4

    edge computing, 16–21

    edge devices, 7

    heterogeneity, 4

    IIoT platforms (*see* Industrial
        Internet of Things (IIoT))

    interfacing mechanism, 28–32

    requirement of, 6

    sensors/actuators, 7

    software, 32–39

L

LoRa protocol design, 25

Low-level data transmission
    protocols

    commercial/industrial
        systems, 25

    inter-board protocols, 24, 25

    intra-board wired
        protocols, 22–24

    wired connections, 22

    wireless communications, 22

M, N

MariaDB

    external storage setup

        database
            directory, 222, 223

        empty database, 222

        folder layout, 221

        formatting data, 218

        hard drive/SSD, 214

        mount option, 219

        partition creation, 216, 217

        partition table creation, 216

        Raspberry Pi mounted
            drives, 220

    store data

        CREATE INDEX
            command, 227

        DESCRIBE command, 226

        index creation, 227

        meters table properties, 226

metrics table creation, 225
onoff table creation, 227
smartpower
database, 224
table structure, 225
MariaDB data source, 274
database component, 274
home dashboard, 276
SELECT, 275
shell command, 274
source setup, 276
Modbus protocol, 27
MQ Telemetry Transport
(MQTT), 27

O

OPC UA data model, 230
ProSys client display, 234
server source code, 231–233
template, 231
Open Platform Communication –
Unified Architecture (OPC
UA), 28, 165
architecture, 166
commander, 189–191
data model editor, 182
data types, 183, 184
node-opcua, 181
ProSys OPC UA client, 191, 192
server, 185–189
data model, 186, 189
variables, 184, 185

P, Q

Physical controls, 30
Plotting system
components, 266
data manipulation, 265
Docker installation, 267–269
Grafana (*see* Grafana)
Power over Ethernet (PoE), 210
Profinet, 25
Programmable logic controllers
(PLC), 20–22

R

Radio-frequency identification
(RFID), 15
Raspberry Pi
camera module, 130, 131
Compute Module 3+, 18
deploy application
LED blinking, 65
onoff library, 65
package manager location, 64
edge computing, 17–19
Model B, 48–51
programmable logic
controller, 20–22
software characteristics, 32
Wyliodrin STUDIO
(*see* Wyliodrin STUDIO)
Real-time response, 33
Representational state transfer
(REST) API, 31, 32

S, T

Serial Peripheral Interface (SPI), 23
Soda dispenser system
  application, 111
    pins setup, 111, 112
  components, 96, 97
  dashboard creation
    live dashboard, 123
    tank widget properties, 122
    variables, 120, 121
  external module, 107, 108
  historical data, 96
  Internet connection, 113
    components, 113
    dashboard creation, 120–123
    liquid amount, 117–120
    ubidots account, 114, 115
    widget values, 115–117
  modules, 113
  pump circuit schematic, 109, 110
  UI (*see* User interface (UI))
  vending machine, 95
  widget values
    characteristics, 116
    elements, 115
    request message, 116
    ubidots configuration, 116
Software
  characteristics of, 32–34
  developing applications
    desktop/web applications, 34
    development
      environments, 36–38
    hardware characteristics, 34
    programming languages,
      35, 36
    user interface, 34
    Wyliodrin STUDIO, 38
Supervisory Control and Data
    Acquisition (SCADA), 10, 11

U, V

Universal Asynchronous Receiver/
    Transmitter (UART), 23
User interface (UI)
  commercial products, 29
  touchscreen, 29
  web application, 29

W, X, Y

Wyliodrin STUDIO
  browser version
    boot partition, 59
    device connection, 58–60
    structure information, 58
    wyliodrin.json file, 57, 59
  connection process
    browser version, 57–60
    credentials suggestion, 57
    Etcher download, 54
    Ethernet connection, 55
    flashing process, 55
    local version, 56, 57
    manual setup, 55
    operating system, 53

requirement, 53
web site, 54
embedded devices, 50
integrated development
    environment, 50
interface, 60
local version, 51
operations, 60
running options
    AppImage file, 52

browser, 53
local version/web version, 52
software development, 38
stores projects, 51
tab options, 61
web version, 51

Z

Zigbee protocol, 26

Printed in the United States
By Bookmasters